Zachariah Allen

**The conditions of life, habits, and customs, of the native Indians of America, and their treatment by the first settlers**

Zachariah Allen

**The conditions of life, habits, and customs, of the native Indians of America, and their treatment by the first settlers**

ISBN/EAN: 9783337305246

Printed in Europe, USA, Canada, Australia, Japan

Cover: Foto ©ninafisch / pixelio.de

More available books at **www.hansebooks.com**

# PROCEEDINGS

OF THE

# Rhode Island Historical Society,

1879-80.

16610

PROVIDENCE:
PRINTED FOR THE SOCIETY.
1880.

# OFFICERS

#### OF THE

## RHODE ISLAND HISTORICAL SOCIETY.

#### ELECTED JANUARY 13TH, 1880.

---

*President.*

SAMUEL G. ARNOLD,* - - - - - PORTSMOUTH.

*Vice Presidents.*

ZACHARIAH ALLEN, - - - - - PROVIDENCE.
FRANCIS BRINLEY, - - - - NEWPORT.

*Secretary.*

AMOS PERRY, - - - - - - PROVIDENCE.

*Treasurer.*

RICHMOND P. EVERETT, - - - - PROVIDENCE.

*Librarian and Cabinet Keeper of the Northern Department.*

EDWIN M. STONE, - - - - - PROVIDENCE.

* Deceased since annual meeting.

### Committee on Nomination of New Members.

| | |
|---|---|
| ALBERT V. JENKS, - - - - - | PROVIDENCE. |
| WILLIAM STAPLES, - - - - - | PROVIDENCE. |
| W. MAXWELL GREENE, - - - - | PROVIDENCE. |

### Committee on Lectures and Reading of Papers.

| | |
|---|---|
| WILLIAM GAMMELL, - - - - - | PROVIDENCE. |
| AMOS PERRY, - - - - - - | PROVIDENCE. |
| CHARLES W. PARSONS, - - - - | PROVIDENCE. |

### Committee on Publications of the Society.

| | |
|---|---|
| JOHN R. BARTLETT, - - - - - | PROVIDENCE. |
| J. LEWIS DIMAN, - - - - - | PROVIDENCE. |
| EDWIN M. STONE, - - - - - | PROVIDENCE. |

### Committee on Genealogical Researches.

| | |
|---|---|
| HENRY E. TURNER, - - - - | NEWPORT. |
| ZACHARIAH ALLEN, - - - - - | PROVIDENCE. |
| WILLIAM A. MOWRY, - - - - - | PROVIDENCE. |

### Committee on Care of Grounds and Building.

| | |
|---|---|
| ISAAC H. SOUTHWICK, - - - - | PROVIDENCE. |
| HENRY J. STEERE, - - - - - | PROVIDENCE. |
| ROYAL C. TAFT, - - - - - | PROVIDENCE. |

### Audit Committee.

| | |
|---|---|
| HENRY T. BECKWITH, - - - - | PROVIDENCE. |
| WALTER BLODGET, - - - - - | PROVIDENCE. |
| JOHN P. WALKER, - - - - - | PROVIDENCE. |

### Procurators.

| | |
|---|---|
| GEORGE C. MASON, - - - - - | NEWPORT. |
| WILLIAM J MILLER, - - - - | BRISTOL. |
| ERASTUS RICHARDSON, - - - - | WOONSOCKET. |
| HENRY F. SMITH, - - - - - | PAWTUCKET. |
| CHARLES H. FISHER, - - - - | SCITUATE. |
| GEORGE H. OLNEY, - - - - - | HOPKINTON. |

# HONORARY MEMBERS.

### Elected since January 1st, 1873.

(For complete list previous to this date see Proceedings for 1872-73.)

| | | |
|---|---|---|
| July 1, 1873. | *William Cullen Bryant, LL. D., | New York City. |
| Oct. 7, 1873. | †Hon. John Lothrop Motley, LL. D., | London, Eng. |
| Jan. 20, 1874. | James Anthony Froude, F. Ex. Col. Ox., | " " |
| Nov. 10, 1874. | ‡Hon. Brantz Mayer, | Baltimore, Md. |
| Oct. 2, 1877. | Hon. Marshall P. Wilder, | Boston, Mass. |
| Oct. 1, 1878. | Don Jose Maria Latino Coelho, Sec. Royal Academy Sciences, | Lisbon, Portugal. |
| April 1, 1879. | Hon. Charles Francis Adams, | Cambridge, Mass. |
| July 1, 1879. | Prof. K. Gislason, Sec. Royal Society Northern Antiquaries, | Copenhagen, Den. |
| Jan. 13, 1880. | Hon. Carl Schurz, Sec. Interior, | Washington, D. C. |

\* Deceased, 1878.  † Deceased, 1877.  ‡ Deceased, 1879.

# CORRESPONDING MEMBERS.

### Elected since April 1st, 1873.

(For complete list previous to this date see Proceedings for 1872-73.)

---

| | | |
|---|---|---|
| July 1, 1873. | Rev. Thomas T. Stone, | Bolton, Mass. |
| Oct. 7, 1873. | Col. Albert H. Hoyt, | Cincinnati, O. |
| " " | William Chambers, LL. D., | Edinburgh, Scotland. |
| " " | Prof. J. C. Holst, | Christiania, Norway. |
| " " | G. J. Bowles, Esq., | Quebec, Canada. |
| Jan. 20, 1874. | Frederick Kidder, Esq., | Boston, Mass. |
| April 7, 1874. | William J. Hoppin, Esq., | New York City. |
| July 7, 1874. | Hon. William Greenough, | Boston, Mass. |
| " " | Rev. Samuel Osgood, D. D., | New York City. |
| " " | Col. John Ward, | " " " |
| " " | Alexander Duncan, Esq., | England. |
| Nov. 10, 1874. | Lyman C. Draper, Esq., | Madison, Wis. |
| April 6, 1875. | Col. Percy Daniel, | Worcester, Mass. |
| " " | Charles H. Russell, Esq., | New York City. |
| " " | Hon. J. Carson Brevoort, | " " " |
| July 6, 1875. | Thomas F. Rowland, Esq., | Brooklyn, N. Y. |
| " " | C. Mason Kinne, Esq., | San Francisco, Cal. |
| Oct. 5, 1875. | Franklin B. Hough, M. D., | Lowville, N. Y. |
| " " | Edmund B. O'Calligan, LL. D., | New York City. |
| " " | Benjamin Greene Arnold, | " " " |
| Jan. 18, 1876. | Marcus D. Gilman, Esq., Lib. Vt. Historical Society, | Montpelier, Vt. |
| " " | Silas Bonfils, Esq., | Mentone, France. |

## CORRESPONDING MEMBERS.

| Date | Name | Location |
|---|---|---|
| Jan. 18, 1876. | Phineas Bates, Jr., Esq., | Boston, Mass. |
| " " | W. Elliott Woodward, Esq., | " " |
| Oct. 3, 1876. | Rt. Rev. M. A. DeWolf Howe, | Reading, Pa. |
| " " | Hon. John S. Brayton, | Fall River, Mass. |
| April 3, 1877. | Hon. Richard A. Wheeler, | Stonington, Conn. |
| April 24, 1877. | Rev. Elmer H. Capen, D. D., | Somerville, Mass. |
| Jan. 15, 1878. | Asa Bird Gardner, LL. D., Prof. U. S. Military Academy, | West Point. |
| " " | Major-Gen. George W. Cullum, U. S. A., | New York City. |
| " " | Brig.-Gen. A. A. Humphreys, Chief Eng Depart., U. S. A., | Washington, D. C. |
| Oct. 1, 1878. | Hon. Isaac N. Arnold, Prest. Chicago Hist Society, | Chicago, Ill. |
| " " | Hiram A. Huse, Esq., Lib. Vt. State Library, | Montpelier, Vt. |
| April 2, 1878. | Gen. Heussein Tevflk, | Constantinople. |
| " " | Hon. John Fitch, | New York City. |
| " " | Edward F. DeLancey, Esq., | " " " |
| Jan. 14, 1879. | Rev. Charles Rogers, LL. D., Sec. Royal Hist. Society, | London, Eng. |
| " " | Col. Thos. Wentworth Higginson, | Cambridge, Mass. |
| " " | Hon. Thomas C. Amory, | Boston, Mass. |
| April 1, 1879. | Ray Greene Huling, | Fitchburg, Mass. |
| " " | A. W. Holden, M. D., | Glen Falls, N. Y. |
| July 1, 1879. | Lt.-Col. Thos. L. Casey, U. S. A., | Washington, D. C. |
| " " | Hon. Edouard Madier de Montjau, Prest. Soc. Ethnology Am., | Paris, France. |
| Jan. 13, 1880. | Prof. Moses Coit Tyler, | Ann Arbor, Michigan. |
| " " | Samuel Dunster, Esq., | East Attleboro, Mass. |

# RESIDENT MEMBERS.

## 1880.

#### Reported by the Treasurer.

| ELECTED. | | ELECTED. | |
|---|---|---|---|
| 1876. | Adams, Charles P. | 1878. | Bogman, Edward Y. |
| 1874. | Addeman, Joshua M. | 1872. | Bowen, Holder B. |
| 1874. | Aldrich, Nelson W. | 1846. | Bradley, Charles S. |
| 1822. | Allen, Zachariah | 1880. | Brayton, William D. |
| 1875. | Ames, William | 1870. | Brinley, Francis |
| 1875. | Angell, Albert G. | 1875. | Brown, John A. |
| 1876. | Angell, Edwin G. | 1857. | Brown, Welcome O. |
| 1836. | Anthony, Henry B. | 1874. | Brownell, Stephen |
| 1876. | Armstrong, Cyrus C. | 1876. | Bugbee, James H. |
| 1875. | Aplin, Charles | 1878. | Bull, Samuel T. |
| 1874. | Arnold, Olney | 1874. | Burnside, Ambrose E. |
| 1844. | *Arnold, Samuel G. | 1878. | Burrough, Frank M. |
| 1877. | Arnold, Stephen H. | 1880. | Burrows, Daniel |
| 1877. | Babbitt, Edward S. | 1859. | Calder, George B. |
| 1872. | Barrows, Edwin | 1876. | Campbell, Horatio N. |
| 1831. | Bartlett, John R. | 1873. | Carpenter, Charles E. |
| 1876. | Barton, Robert | 1874. | Carpenter, Francis W. |
| 1879. | Barton, William T. | 1874. | Caswell, Edward T. |
| 1849. | Beckwith, Henry T. | 1857. | Chambers, Robert B. |
| 1877. | Bedlow, Henry | 1880. | Chandler, William H. |
| 1858. | Binney, William | 1872. | Channing, William F. |
| 1873. | Blodget, Walter | 1879. | Chace, Lewis J. |

\* Deceased, February 13, 1870.

## RESIDENT MEMBERS. 9

| ELECTED. | | ELECTED. | |
|---|---|---|---|
| 1868. | Chace, Thomas W. | 1874. | Fairbrother, Henry L. |
| 1873. | Claflin, George L. | 1878. | Farnsworth, Claudius B. |
| 1880. | Clarke, E. Webster | 1876. | Fay, Henry H. |
| 1878. | Clarke, James M. | 1878. | Fisher, Charles H. |
| 1873. | Clarke, Sam W. | 1855. | Gammell, Asa Messer |
| 1878. | Clark, Thomas M. | 1875. | Gammell, Robert Ives |
| 1879. | Clarke, William E. | 1844. | Gammell, William |
| 1880. | Coats, James | 1875. | Gardner, Henry W. |
| 1877. | Codman, Arthur | 1880. | Goddard, Francis W. |
| 1879. | Colt, LeBaron B. | 1850. | Goddard, William |
| 1879. | Colt, Samuel P. | 1878. | Godding, Alvah W. |
| 1877. | Conant, Hezekiah | 1858. | Gorham, John |
| 1872. | Congdon, Johns H. | 1878. | Gorton, Charles |
| 1872. | Cooke, Joseph J. | 1878. | Greene, Edward A. |
| 1874. | Cranston, Henry C. | 1876. | Greene, Henry L. |
| 1877. | Cranston, George K. | 1874. | Greene, Simon Henry |
| 1879. | Cross, William J. | 1866. | Greene, William |
| 1876. | Cushman, Henry I. | 1877. | Greene, W. Maxwell |
| 1874. | Day, Daniel E. | 1879. | Greer, David H. |
| 1871. | Dean, Sidney | 1872. | Grosvenor, William |
| 1879. | DeWolf, Winthrop | 1872. | Grosvenor, William Jr. |
| 1874. | Dike, Arba B. | 1878. | Hall, Robert |
| 1866. | Diman, J. Lewis | 1879. | Hammond, Benjamin B. |
| 1877. | Doringh, Charles H. R. | 1878. | Harkness, Albert |
| 1877. | Dorrance, Samuel R. | 1874. | Harrington, Henry A. |
| 1836. | Dorrance, William T. | 1878. | Harris, C. Fiske |
| 1851. | Doyle, Thomas A. | 1877. | Hartshorn, Joseph C. |
| 1875. | Dunnell, William Wanton | 1836. | Hazard, Rowland G. |
| 1877. | Durfee, Charles S. | 1871. | Hazard, Rowland |
| 1849. | Durfee, Thomas | 1873. | Hidden, Henry A. |
| 1838. | Dyer, Elisha | 1873. | Hidden, James C. |
| 1873. | Eames, Benjamin T. | 1874. | Hill, Thomas J. |
| 1872. | Eaton, Amasa M. | 1874. | Holbrook, Albert |
| 1878. | Elliott, Albert T. | 1874. | Hopkins, William H. |
| 1876. | Ely, James W. C. | 1871. | Hoppin, Frederick S. |
| 1862. | Ely, William D. | 1880. | Howard, Albert C. |
| 1876. | Ely, William | 1843. | Howland, John A. |
| 1858. | Everett, Richmond P. | 1867. | Jenks, Albert V. |

## RHODE ISLAND HISTORICAL SOCIETY.

ELECTED.
1879. Jillson, Charles D.
1874. Johnson, William S.
1879. Johnson, Elias H.
1880. Jones, Augustine
1867. Keene, Stephen S.
1873. Kendall, Henry L.
1876. Kimball, James M.
1879. Knight, Edward B.
1876. Knowles, Edward P.
1869. Lester, John Erastus
1879. Lincoln, John L.
1880. Lippitt, Christopher
1878. Lippitt, C. Warren
1872. Lippitt, Henry
1879. Lockwood, Amos D.
1873. Lyman, Daniel W.
1877. Mason, Charles F.
1877. Mason, Earl Philip
1877. Mason, Eugene W.
1877. Mason, George C.
1876. Matteson, Charles
1878. Mauran, Edward C.
1878. Mauran, James E.
1867. Meader, John J.
1876. Metcalf, Henry B., Pawtucket.
1875. Miller, Augustus S.
1873. Miller, William J.
1876. Moulton, Sullivan
1873. Mowry, William A.
1874. Mowry, William G. R.
1877. Mumford, John P.
1877. Munroe, Bennett J.
1880. Munroe, Wilfred H.
1880. Nichols, Amos G.
1876. Nickerson, Edward I.
1874. Nightingale, George C. Jr.
1865. *Oldfield, John

ELECTED.
1879. Olney, George H.
1862. Ormsbee, John Spurr
1878. Owen, Smith
1870. Pabodie, Benjamin F.
1874. †Pabodie, Benjamin G.
1874. Paige, Charles F.
1867. Paine, George T.
1867. Parkhurst, Jonathan G.
1847. Parsons, Charles W.
1875. Parsons, Henry L.
1873. Pearce, Edward
1877. Pearce, Edward D. Jr.
1849. Peckham, Samuel W.
1875. Pegram, John C.
1858. Perry, Amos
1880. Perry, Marsden J.
1874. Persons, Benjamin W.
1873. Philips, Theodore W.
1878. Porter, Emery H.
1880. Potter, Charles L.
1876. Rawson, Henry M.
1874. Richardson, Erastus
1877. Richmond, Walter
1878. Rider, Sidney S.
1866. Rogers, Horatio
1878. Russell, Levi W.
1877. Seabury, Frederic N.
1877. Seagraves, Caleb
1874. Shaw, James Jr.
1875. Sherman, William O.
1874. Shedd, J. Herbert
1879. Shepley, George H.
1876. Sherman, Robert
1877. Slater, Horatio N. Jr.
1876. Slater, William S.
1875. Smith, Edwin A.
1873. Smith, Henry F.

* Deceased, January 8, 1880.   † Deceased, January 25, 1880.

## RESIDENT MEMBERS.

ELECTED.
- 1869. Southwick, Isaac H.
- 1874. Spencer, Gideon L.
- 1876. Spencer, Joel M.
- 1877. Stanhope, Frederick A.
- 1873. Staples, Carlton A.
- 1869. Staples, William
- 1878. Starkweather, Joseph U.
- 1868. Steere, Henry J.
- 1879. Stiness, John H.
- 1848. Stone, Edwin M.
- 1873. Swan, Jarvis B.
- 1856. Taft, Royal C.
- 1874. Taylor, Charles F.
- 1878. Tillinghast, James
- 1879. Tibbitts, William T.

ELECTED.
- 1877. Thayer, Thatcher
- 1873. Thurston, Benjamin F.
- 1875. Trippe, Samuel G.
- 1874. Turner, Henry E.
- 1874. Wales, Samuel H.
- 1874. Walker, John P.
- 1861. Waterman, Rufus
- 1878. Watson, Arthur H.
- 1868. Weeden, William B.
- 1868. Westcott, Amasa S.
- 1874. Whitford, George W.
- 1877. Wilson, George F.
- 1876. Woods, Marshall
- 1880. Woodward, Royal

# LIFE MEMBERS.

| | | |
|---|---|---|
| Jan. 16, 1872. | George T. Paine, | Providence. |
| Jan. 17, 1872. | Henry T. Beckwith, | " |
| Feb. 21, 1872. | William Greene, | Warwick. |
| April 3, 1872. | Rowland G. Hazard, | South Kingstown. |
| April 25, 1872. | Holder Borden Bowen, | Providence. |
| July 11, 1872. | Amasa M. Eaton, | North Providence. |
| Jan. 29, 1873. | James Y. Smith,* | Providence. |
| July 11, 1873. | Jarvis B. Swan, | " |
| Jan. 26, 1874. | Benjamin G. Pabodie,* | " |
| April 12, 1875. | Albert G. Angell. | " |
| Jan. 29, 1876. | William Ely, | " |
| April 11, 1877. | Hezekiah Conant, | Pawtucket. |
| Jan. 14, 1879. | Samuel G. Arnold,* | Portsmouth. |
| July 8, 1879. | Amos D. Lockwood. | Providence. |
| Oct. 16, 1879. | Royal Woodward, | Albany, N. Y. |
| Jan. 7, 1880. | Charles Gorton, | Providence. |

* Deceased.

# PROCEEDINGS

OF THE

# RHODE ISLAND HISTORICAL SOCIETY.

## SPECIAL MEETING.

PROVIDENCE, January 28, 1879.

A meeting was held this evening at 7¾ o'clock, Vice President Allen in the chair.

A note was read from the Librarian, who was detained by indisposition, announcing numerous donations made since the last meeting, among which was a piece of the first Atlantic Cable, with an original letter from Cyrus W. Field, presented by Christopher Burr, Esq.

Hon. Abraham Payne then addressed the Society on the Life and Times of Jonathan Edwards. Mr. Payne stated, at the outset, that his object was not to present a sketch of this most remarkable theologian, but simply to awaken interest in his writings. He spoke for upwards of an hour, enlisting the close attention of his auditors.

At the conclusion of his address, Rev. Mr. Staples related several striking anecdotes illustrative of the eloquence and earnestness of the great divine, and concluded his remarks by offering a resolution thanking Mr. Payne for his eloquent and interesting discourse, which resolution was seconded by Hon. Thomas A. Doyle, and after some spirited remarks by Vice President Allen, was unanimously passed.

Col. John Ward, of New York, was announced to read the next paper on the 11th of February.

The meeting was numerously attended, and the exercises passed off in a most satisfactory manner.

Adjourned.

Amos Perry, Sec'y.

## SPECIAL MEETING.

Providence, February 11, 1879.

A meeting was held this evening to hear a paper read by Col. John Ward, of New York, Vice President Allen in the chair.

A list of donations received since the last meeting was read by the Secretary. Besides twenty books and pamphlets was a relic of slavery in the form of a slave chain taken from the body of a negro who was found chained with it to a tree on the plantations of Mr. Belson, near Simmsport, Louisiana, in May, 1863, by Capt. Peter Brucker, of the Second Rhode Island Cavalry, and by him presented to the Society.

Col. John Ward read a graphic and succinct account of the Siege of Harper's Ferry by Stonewall Jackson in 1862.

The reading occupied an hour and a half, and was listened to with profound attention.

On motion of Prof. Diman, Col. Ward received a unanimous vote of thanks for the highly interesting paper. In offering the resolution, Prof. Diman paid a marked compliment to the lecturer, and Vice President Allen added his word of commendation.

Notwithstanding the rain-storm the room was well filled.

Dr. Henry E. Turner, of Newport, was announced to read the next paper on the 25th inst., to which time the meeting was adjourned.

AMOS PERRY, *Sec'y*.

## SPECIAL MEETING.

PROVIDENCE, February 25, 1879.

A meeting was held this evening at a quarter before eight o'clock, Vice President Allen in the chair.

Dr. Henry E. Turner read a paper on Jeremiah Clarke and his descendants, showing this family to have been remarkable for the number of governors and deputy-governors it has furnished the State, and for the wide diffusion of its blood through the old colonial families of various names. The paper evinced extensive and thorough historical research, and threw much light on a portion of our history pertaining to the period of the Sir Edmond Andros usurpation. It vividly portrayed some of the leading characters of the Jeremiah Clarke family, and set forth in a clear light the principles of the opposing factions in the State.

At the close of the reading, which occupied an hour and a half, some spirited and highly complimentary remarks were offered by Messrs. Denison, Allen and Perry, and a unanimous vote of thanks was passed to Dr. Turner for his exhaustive and instructive address, which, it was remarked, should be printed and widely circulated.

Notice was given that John Austin Stevens, Esquire, Editor of the *Magazine of American History*, would read the next paper, March 11, on the French in Rhode Island.

The meeting was then adjourned.

AMOS PERRY, *Sec'y*.

## SPECIAL MEETING.

PROVIDENCE, March 11, 1879.

A special meeting was held this evening. Vice President Allen in the chair.

The record of the last meeting was read and approved. Also, a list of contributions received by the Librarian was read.

John Austin Stevens, Esquire, Editor of the *Magazine of American History*, was then introduced and proceeded to read a paper on the French in Rhode Island during our Revolutionary War. Opening with expressions of satisfaction that the French nation has established a republican form of government. Mr. Stevens proceeded to give a full and exceedingly interesting history of the French troops in Rhode Island from the organization and arrival of the first expedition under Count d'Estaing to aid the United States in establishing their independence, till the departure of the second expedition under Count Rochambeau, after the surrender of Cornwallis at Yorktown, which closed the Revolutionary War.

The paper gave a detailed account of the French occupation of our State and of their military and civic relations with the government and the people, and more especially with the inhabitants of Newport and Providence, by whom the French allies were warmly welcomed as the friends of our republic, then struggling into existence, and entertained with a cordial and generous hospitality as champions of the American cause. Personal sketches were also given of prominent French officers of both expeditions and of many political and social movements and events with which they were connected during their residence in this State and country.

The Historical Cabinet was filled with an audience of ladies and gentlemen who listened to the reading of the paper with deep interest.

Mr. Stevens received the thanks of the Society, embodied in a resolution offered by Rt. Rev. Thomas M. Clark and seconded by Prof. J. Lewis Diman. Some highly interesting reminiscences were added by Vice President Allen, and critical remarks by Messrs. Clark, Diman and Denison.

Adjourned.

AMOS PERRY, Sec'y.

## QUARTERLY MEETING.

PROVIDENCE, April 1, 1879.

The quarterly meeting of the Society was held this evening, at a quarter before eight o'clock, Vice President Allen in the chair.

The Secretary read the record of the last meeting and of the last annual meeting. He also announced the reception of letters from Don Jose Maria Latino Coellio, Secretary of the Royal Academy of Sciences of Lisbon, Portugal, accepting with thanks his election as an honorary member; and from Hon. Thomas C. Amory, of Boston, his election as a corresponding member of the Society. The Secretary then laid before the Society the following communication:

PROVIDENCE, R. I., April 1, 1879.

*Mr. Amos Perry, Secretary R. I. Historical Society:*

DEAR SIR:—I hereby present, through you, to the Rhode Island Historical Society the accompanying watch, which was the property of my late husband, Captain Joseph Herlitz, Commander of the great ship Ganges, when she was driven up to the head of the Cove by the great gale of September 23, 1815. It was worn by him at that time. It has always been an excellent time keeper, and in running order up to a recent time, when it was injured by some repairs.

Its manufacturer was Richard Farrell, of Dublin, Ireland, and it came into my husband's possession at the close of a voyage,—a gift from the owner of the vessel. Since his death, December 18, 1817, it has naturally been a most precious memento to me of by-gone days and events, and now feeling the thread of life to be nearly run,—being in my eighty-third year,—I desire to deposit the watch in the safe keeping of your honorable Society, that it may be handed down to future generations as an interesting relic and memorial of olden times.

I am respectfully yours,

LOUISA (LIPPITT) HERLITZ.

The following resolutions offered by Rev. E. M. Stone, were then unanimously passed:

*Resolved*, That the thanks of this Society are hereby presented to Mrs. Louisa Lippitt Herlitz for the very acceptable donation of a watch, worn by her late husband, Captain Joseph Herlitz, Commander of the great ship Ganges when driven by the great gale of September 23, 1815, and the force of an extraordinary tide, against the Washington Building, and there stranded.

*Resolved*, That in accepting the gift of Mrs Herlitz this Society begs leave to assure her that it shall be preserved with great care among its articles of virtu.

The Librarian announced numerous donations and exchanges since the last meeting.

Mr. R. P. Everett offered the following resolution, which was seconded by Rev. E. M. Stone with a brief eulogy of Mr. Williams, after which it was adopted unanimously :

*Resolved*, That by the death of William Greene Williams, the Society has been deprived of one of its oldest, most active and devoted members, and that in view of his long and useful services, a record of this event be made by the Secretary, and a copy of this resolution be transmitted to the family of the deceased.

Mr. A. V. Jenks, chairman of the Committee on Nomination of New Members, reported in favor of the election of the following gentlemen, and they were accordingly elected:

RESIDENT MEMBERS.— John H. Stiness, Charles D. Jillson, Winthrop DeWolf, Edward B. Knight.

CORRESPONDING MEMBERS.—Ray Greene Huling, Fitchburg, Mass., Dr. A. W. Holden, Glenn's Falls, N. Y.

HONORARY MEMBER.—Hon. Charles Francis Adams, Cambridge, Mass.

Mr. George T. Paine read a detailed report, in behalf of the Committee appointed a year ago to keep the Cabinet open, and prosecute the work of cataloguing the effects of the Society, together with the Act of the General Assembly granting annually to the Society five hundred dollars for the care, preservation and utilization of the State property in charge of the Society. The Act, which was formally accepted, reads as follows :

[*Passed at the January Session, 1879.*]

## CHAPTER 711.

AN ACT IN AMENDMENT OF CHAPTER 24 OF THE GENERAL STATUTES "OF THE STATE LIBRARY."

(Passed March 7, 1879.)

*It is enacted by the General Assembly as follows:*

SECTION 1. The sum of five hundred dollars is annually appropriated, to be expended under the direction of the Rhode Island Historical Society, for the care and preservation and the cataloguing of the property of the State in its keeping, and for purchase and binding of books relating to the history of the State, and for copying and preserving the records in the several towns of the State.

SEC. 2. The Rhode Island Historical Society shall annually, at the May session, make report to the General Assembly of the manner in which the above appropriation has been expended.

SEC. 3. All books and papers belonging to the State, in the keeping of the Rhode Island Historical Society, or which may be purchased under the above appropriation, shall be plainly marked as the property of the State, and shall at all seasonable times be for the use of the citizens of the State.

SEC. 4. This act shall take effect from and after its passage.

The report was accepted, and the following resolution, recommended by the Committee, was then adopted:

*Resolved,* That ———— ———— be a Committee who shall arrange with the General Treasurer for the payment of the money appropriated by the Legislature of the State to the annual use of the Historical Society, and shall, in their discretion, disburse the same in accordance with the provisions of the act.

Messrs. John H. Stiness, Charles W. Parsons and George T. Paine were nominated and elected as the Committee provided for by the above resolution.

A recommendation for the appointment of a Committee on Criticism failed to pass.

Mr. George T. Paine offered several proposed amendments to the Constitution, which were read, and continued for action to the next quarterly meeting in July.

On motion of Mr. Amos Perry, the thanks of the Society were voted to the Special Committee, for their extended, efficient and satisfactory work in reorganizing and cataloguing the Library and keeping it open and accessible.

Mr. A. V. Jenks nominated Mr. William Maxwell Greene as a member of the Committee on the Nomination of New Members, in place of William Greene Williams, deceased, and he was elected.

Mr. R. P. Everett offered the following resolution, which was read and passed:

*Resolved*, That five hundred copies of the Reports of the Librarian, Treasurer, and various Standing Committees, together with the Proceedings of 1878-9, be printed for the use of the members, the cost of the same not to exceed one hundred and fifty dollars.

The following named gentlemen were nominated and elected:

PROCURATORS.—George C. Mason, Newport; William J. Miller, Bristol; Erastus Richardson, Woonsocket; Henry F. Smith, Pawtucket; Dr. Charles H Fisher, Scituate; George H. Olney, Hopkinton.

On motion, the meeting was then adjourned.

AMOS PERRY, *Sec'y*.

## SPECIAL MEETING.

PROVIDENCE, May 20, 1879.

A meeting was held this evening, the President in the chair, to hear a paper read by Rev. George E. Ellis, D. D., of Boston, on "The Present Indian Question with our Government."

The high reputation of Dr. Ellis as a writer, together with a warm interest in the subject of his paper, drew together a numerous and eager audience. At the beginning of the discussion Dr. Ellis repeated, as a guiding principle, the quaint adage that no question is settled until it is rightly settled. The discourse was the fruit of a vigorous and well-trained mind, thoroughly enlisted in the discussion of a grave and practical subject, and its author received at the conclusion of the reading, on motion of Prof. J. Lewis Diman, seconded by Hon. John R. Bartlett, the unanimous thanks of the Society. One of the conclusions reached by Dr. Ellis, and urged as the key to all right action in the premises, was, that our Government is the guardian of the Indians and, conversely, that the Indians are the wards of the Government. On this point he spoke with positiveness, bewailing the evils that have resulted from mixed systems and confused ideas. To longer waver here is, he said, both a folly and a crime. The guardian must exercise good faith, decision and energy, and at the same time must insist that his wards shall have fixed habitations and shall cultivate such habits of industry as tend to Christian civilization. Without disparaging the War Department, he insisted on the exercise of moral force, and especially on fairness and honesty in our dealings with these children of the forest. He denounced as barbarous and heathenish, the doctrine of extermination, understood to be favored by some citizens outside our military ranks. The general tenor of the discourse was pronounced by Prof. Diman to be in accord with the teachings of Roger Williams and John Elliot, whose apostolic character has received the sanction of the present generation.

On motion, the meeting was adjourned.

AMOS PERRY, *Sec'y*.

## QUARTERLY MEETING.

PROVIDENCE, July 1, 1879.

The regular quarterly meeting was held this afternoon at 3 o'clock, the President in the chair.

The record of the last quarterly meeting was read and approved.

A letter was also read from Hon. Charles Francis Adams accepting the office of honorary member of the Society, and expressing an interest in the objects proposed. The Secretary also gave an abstract of letters from Mr. Ray Greene Huling, of Fitchburg, Mass., acknowledging the honor of his election as corresponding member, and expressing his readiness to co-operate in promoting the objects of the Society.

The Librarian reported numerous valuable donations made since the last quarterly meeting, among which was the Whitney Genealogy, consisting of three superbly bound and illustrated volumes, presented by J. Whitney Phœnix, of New York. This generous donation called forth warm expressions of appreciation and of gratitude to the donor, though no formal vote was passed.

The Committee on the Nomination of New Members recommended, through Mr. A. V. Jenks, the following persons for membership, and they were accordingly elected:

RESIDENT MEMBERS.—Rev. C. A. L. Richards, Rev. E. H. Johnson, D. D., Rev. D. H. Greer and Amos D. Lockwood, Esq.

HONORARY MEMBER.—Prof. K. Gislason, Secretary of the Royal Society of Northern Antiquaries, Copenhagen, Denmark.

The Secretary laid before the Society a letter from the Hon. John H. Stiness tendering to the Society the resignation of his office as a member of the Special Committee to carry out the State Appropriation Act. After due consideration the motion was made and passed that Vice President Allen be appointed a Committee to confer with Judge Stiness and request him to favor the Society with his continued services as a member of the above named Committee.

The amendments to the Constitution, proposed at the last quarterly meeting and referred for action to the present meeting, were taken up and discussed section by section. The section proposing to have a standing committee to be called "A Library Committee," and the section defining the duties of this committee, were laid upon the table to be called up for action at the next annual meeting. All the other proposed amendments were indefinitely postponed.

Mr. Henry T. Beckwith received permission to take from the library, under the usual restrictions, a certain book, for the purpose of having a picture therein copied.

A resolution was offered and seconded, having for its object the prevention of hasty action in stamping the seal of the State on the Society's collections. After the manifestation of a lively interest on the subject the resolution was withdrawn.

A report from the Special Committee appointed at the last quarterly meeting to carry out the General Assembly grant of money was called for. The Committee had reported to the General Assembly, and, probably by oversight, had failed to account to the Society to which it is primarily responsible. Vice President Allen was appointed a Committee to look after this branch of business.

Mr. Edward S. Babbitt gave, by invitation, an extended

account of the proposed bi-centennial celebration at Bristol during the coming year, and near the close of his remarks, which were listened to with lively interest, invited the co-operation and friendly aid of the Society in bringing about the proposed re-union and jubilee.

Mr. Babbitt's glowing account and earnest appeal drew forth a prompt response by Mr. Perry, who expressed, in behalf of the Society, a hearty appreciation of the historic movement in the town of Bristol, and at the conclusion of his remarks, offered the following resolution :

*Resolved*, That learning this afternoon of the proposed bi-centennial observance in Bristol, the Historical Society seizes the occasion to send words of greeting to that delightful historic town upon Narragansett and Mt. Hope Bays, expressing a lively interest in the proposed celebration, and proffering such co-operation and aid as are in its power.

The resolution was seconded by Prof. J. Lewis Diman, and after calling forth cordial expressions of interest from Messrs. Diman, Stone, Allen and Southwick, was unanimously adopted.

Mr. Bennet J. Munro, the veteran journalist, and an authoritative antiquarian of Bristol, responded in brief terms to some enquiries about the early history of his native town.

On motion, the meeting was adjourned.

AMOS PERRY, *Sec'y.*

## QUARTERLY MEETING.

PROVIDENCE, October 7, 1879.

The meeting was called to order at a quarter before eight

o'clock, when, Vice President Allen not having arrived, Hon. John R. Bartlett was called to the chair.

The record of the last meeting was read.

The Librarian reported the donations received since the last meeting, consisting of 239 pamphlets, 78 bound volumes, 25 volumes of newspapers, 13 unbound volumes of books, 3 maps, 19 single papers, and other smaller contributions.

The Secretary read an extract from a private letter written by the President of the Society expressing regret that serious indisposition compelled him to abandon the intention of attending either of the meetings this week.

The Secretary also read a communication from Mr. William H. Spooner, Secretary of the Bi-Centennial Committee of Bristol, gratefully acknowledging the action taken by this Society at the last quarterly meeting in reference to their proposed bi-centennial observance.

The Secretary reported that Judge Stiness had consented to yield to the request of the Society to serve on the Committee appointed at the April quarterly meeting.

A copy of the report made to the General Assembly at the last May session by the Committee appointed to carry out the provisions of the State Appropriation Act, was read and received.

The Committee on the Nomination of New Members reported through their chairman, Mr. A. V. Jenks. Their report was received and adopted, the election resulting as follows:

RESIDENT MEMBERS.—William J. Cross, William T. Barton.

CORRESPONDING MEMBERS.—Lt.-Col. Thomas L. Casey, U. S. A., Washington, D. C ; Hon. Edouard Madier de Montjau, President de la Societe Ethnologique Americaine, Paris, France.

LIFE MEMBER.— Royal Woodward, Esq., Albany, N. Y.

Mr. Woodward has the honor of being the first non-resident life member ever elected by the Society, this action resulting from a letter addressed by him to Rev. E. M. Stone, wherein he expressed a lively interest in the objects of our Society, and suggested that it would afford him pleasure to become a life member. That the compliment thus paid the Society was appreciated by our members was appropriately shown on the occasion, and the desire was expressed that the Secretary should note this fact.

Rev. E. M. Stone offered the following resolution, prefacing it with a brief account of the labors and expense involved in the preparation and publication of the work referred to at the last quarterly meeting:

*Resolved*, That the thanks of this Society are hereby presented to Steven Whitney Phoenix, Esq., of New York, for his munificent gift of three elegantly printed volumes comprising the Genealogy of "the Whitney Family of Connecticut and its affiliations," prepared by himself, a work exhaustive in its character, and a noble monument of his successful endeavors.

The resolution was seconded by Vice President Allen, and after the most cordial endorsement of its sentiments by him, and by Hon. John R. Bartlett, was unanimously passed.

The following resolution was offered by Rev. E. M. Stone, and seconded by Vice President Allen, and after these gentlemen and the chairman of the evening had made remarks showing their high appreciation of the value of the gift, and one of them had stated that probably not another set of the Boston *Liberator* could be had on any terms, the resolution was unanimously passed:

*Resolved*, That the thanks of this Society are hereby presented to Mrs. John Carter Brown for her very acceptable donation to its library of a complete set of the Boston *Liberator*.*

\* When this action took place the set of *Liberators* was supposed to be complete, but on subsequent examination it was ascertained that the first five volumes were wanting.

On motion of Mr. R. P. Everett, the following resolution was unanimously passed :

*Resolved*, That the Society hereby authorizes the purchase of the series of Rider's Historical Tracts, now in the course of publication.

Rev. Mr. Stone asked permission to make a drawing or photograph of the sword and pistols that used to belong to Col. Ephraim Bowen, while in public service during the Revolutionary War. The petitioner's object being to illustrate an important work now in the course of preparation for the press, a vote was promptly taken granting his request.

At this stage in the proceedings the Secretary was called away, and Mr. Edwin Barrows was chosen to discharge his duties till the close of the meeting.

On motion of Mr. George T. Paine, it was

*Voted*, That the expense of heating the room and taking care of it be paid by the Society.

A lengthy, though somewhat informal discussion took place, having for its object to ascertain the true intent and interpretation of the appropriation act of the last General Assembly. The result of the prolonged interview and great freedom of expression was to somewhat harmonize very conflicting views and to moderate, if not remove, fears of serious complications if not of losses entertained by some devoted members of the Society. The Chairman of the Committee on the State appropriation, Judge Stiness, gave his opinion that the Society did not risk losing the control of the books, pamphlets and manuscripts by having them bound at the expense of the State.

Adjourned.

AMOS PERRY, *Sec'y.*

## SPECIAL MEETING.

Providence, October 10, 1879.

The meeting held this evening was called to order at a quarter before eight o'clock by Vice President Allen, who introduced the Hon. Isaac N. Arnold, the President of the Chicago Historical Society, as the speaker of the evening.

Mr. Arnold then rose and gave a discourse upon "Who led the American Troops to Victory in the Northern Campaign of 1777?" occupying more than an hour and a half in the delivery, closely engaging the attention of the audience and throwing much light on certain great military movements and feats of skill and valor, which happening just in the nick of time turned the current of events in favor of the colonists by giving them hope and confidence and bringing to their support powerful French naval and land forces. The portrait of Benedict Arnold was drawn with masterly skill and discrimination. No attempt was made to palliate the traitor's crime. Treason is death to its author, giving him a hue supposed to belong to the dwellers in Tartarus. No colors are too black to be-fit the traitor. The dyes, however, belong only to the period after the evil has been perpetrated. Because Adam sinned we do not refuse to acknowledge his previous innocence. Neither should we refuse to acknowledge Benedict Arnold's good deeds before his fall. His bravery, skill, perseverance and patriotic endeavors are mere matters of history to which we should not be blind. This is simple justice. The difficulty and delicacy of the task undertaken by Mr. Arnold were appreciated by the audience. At the conclusion of the address the Hon. John R. Bartlett made a motion that the thanks of the Society be presented to Mr. Arnold for his paper, evincing thorough research and investigation, good scholarship and sound reasoning, and that a copy of the paper be requested for the archives of the Society, which motion, after being seconded and endorsed by the Secretary and the Chairman, was unanimously passed.

On motion, the meeting was adjourned.

AMOS PERRY, *Sec'y.*

## SPECIAL MEETING.

PROVIDENCE, November 5, 1879.

The meeting was called to order at $7\frac{3}{4}$ o'clock, and in the absence of the President and both Vice Presidents Rev. Carlton A. Staples was elected Chairman.

The Librarian announced 106 donations received since the last meeting; of which 40 were bound volumes, 45 pamphlets, and the remainder newspapers.

A communication from Rev. Frederick Denison was laid before the Society, suggesting that an effort be made to preserve some portion of an old Indian pottery manufacturing establishment, recently brought to light on the farm of Mr. H. N. Angell, in the town of Johnston, and a Committee consisting of Rev. Frederick Denison, Vice President Allen and William G. R. Mowry was appointed to take this matter into consideration, and report at a subsequent meeting.

The Chairman then introduced General Horatio Rogers, who read a paper on La Corne St. Luc, the leader of Burgoyne's Indians. General Rogers first sketched the personnel of Burgoyne's officers, and from their character reasoned that the leader of Burgoyne's Indians would be a man of no common order. He alluded to the feeling of Burgoyne against the employment of Indians in the war against the Colonists,— a feeling which the home government did not respect,— and then gave a brief but comprehensive and exceedingly interesting sketch of La Corne St. Luc. St. Luc had performed eminent civil and military service in Canada before the Revolutionary War. He was an active leader against the English in Canada, but during the Revolutionary struggle he joined hands with his former enemies, the English, who had gained possession of Canada. Disappointed and chagrined he made preparations to leave Canada and reach France with his family and followers, and he set sail, but the vessel was wrecked, his family and most of his followers lost, and after a journey of sixteen hundred and fifty miles, in the severest season of the year, he arrived at Quebec February 23, 1762. The loss of his family and friends changed his plan of life, and he remained in the country. For several years he was Superintendent of the Indians, in Canada, and in 1778 was one of the Legislative Counsellors. When the hostilities between Great Britain and the American Colonies began St. Luc, then sixty-six years old, took up for the Crown, and his partisanship was intensified by a feeling of revenge for ill-treatment at the hands of General Montgomery. The services and atrocities of the Indians, during the campaign under Burgoyne, were described, and the paper closed with a summing up of the character of St. Luc, who was represented as a man of education and civil and military ability, but also as brutal, sanguinary, grasping, avaricious and unprincipled.

The paper was received with marked favor by a highly appreciative audience, and at the conclusion of the reading, on motion of Rev. E. M. Stone, who offered extended remarks on the general subject, the following resolution was unanimously passed:

*Resolved*, That the thanks of this Society are hereby presented to General Horatio Rogers, for the highly interesting and valuable contribution to the military history of the Revolutionary period of the United American Colonies, read this evening, and that a copy of the same be requested for the archives of the Society.

On motion, the meeting was adjourned.

AMOS PERRY, *Sec'y*.

## SPECIAL MEETING.

PROVIDENCE, November 19, 1879.

The meeting was called to order this evening at $7\frac{3}{4}$ o'clock by Vice President Allen, who at once introduced Prof. J. L. Lincoln, LL. D., as the lecturer of the evening. The latter began with the remark that he had had occasion recently to examine the character and works of the Historian Tacitus, and that in this essay it was his aim to set forth the impressions and reflections derived from that careful study. Tacitus needs to be very patiently studied in order to be appreciated. He has never been popular, but in every age he has been admired by a few scholars who have recognized the value of his works, and have found in them useful political lessons. Prof. Lincoln proceeded to review the little that is known of the private and public life of Tacitus. He showed that in the conduct of affairs the historian gained the fame of wisdom, experience and influence, and that like results were won by him as a lawyer. He then referred to his Agricola and Germania, which he regarded as historical studies preparatory to his subsequent works, which, unfortunately, have not been preserved to us entire. Tacitus had to deal with the imperial system. He had to treat of it in fact as well as substance, and as administered in a tyrannical spirit, characterized by frantic excesses and exhibitions of cruelty without parallel. No reader was so well aware of the sober character of his historical task as the writer himself. The process of historical research in the age of Tacitus was not so critical as in modern times. His work consisted, it is probable, not so much in the examination and verification of documents and records as in the sifting and comparing of the works of his predecessors in the line of his studies. Yet we know that he subjected those writers to a searching comparison, and having reached independent conclusions set upon them in his pages the stamp of his own mind. Whatever errors and sins might be laid to him, the unprejudiced reader cannot fail to believe that he was animated by those high moral views which he professed. In all issues where virtue, justice and honor were concerned, attaching to either social or public life, his vision was clear, his heart in the right place. His antipathies were strong against vice of every sort; against all that was low and debasing for a Roman, whether emperor, citizen or magistrate. Yet it must be said he was not free from the prejudices of the Roman nation and the Roman nobles. The essayist went on to speak of the Roman spirit of contempt with which the historian regarded foreigners, of his antipathy to the Jews, of his dislike to the Christians. Yet, it is evident, Tacitus was not always swayed by national feeling, as was evidenced by the admiration with which he regarded the Germans.

After dwelling at some length upon the political principles of Tacitus, his hatred of despotism and tyranny, and his ideas (practical, not visionary) of republicanism in government, Prof. Lincoln spoke of the merits of the great historian as a writer. These were due largely, he said, to the union in him of the powers of thought and reasoning with the gift of careful and vivid description, which always entered largely into his poetic nature. His narrative was clear and strong; his description picturesque and effective. By study and insight he had come to behold distinctly the persons and events of which he wrote in their essential character, and the influences which had made and shaped them, and he set them before the reader so distinctly that all seemed to be present as living realities. In the delineation of character and description of the inner life of men his power was well nigh unrivalled.

At the conclusion of the reading, on motion of Dr. C. W. Parsons, seconded by Rev. E. M. Stone, a unanimous vote of thanks was passed to Prof. Lincoln for his scholarly and elaborate discourse, which drew forth from the mover of the resolution and Vice President Allen pertinent and critical remarks.

Rev. Frederick Denison made an extended report in behalf of the Committee appointed at the last meeting to secure some suitable memorial of the old Indian pottery manufacturing establishment in the town of Johnston. Owing to the lateness of the hour action on the report was deferred till the next meeting, when it was hoped effective measures would be adopted to secure the desired object.

Adjourned to the 22d inst.

AMOS PERRY, *Sec'y.*

## SPECIAL MEETING.

PROVIDENCE, November 22, 1879.

A meeting was held according to appointment at eight

o'clock this evening, but owing to the inconsiderable attendance the meeting was adjourned to the call of the Secretary.

AMOS PERRY, Sec'y.

## SPECIAL MEETING.

PROVIDENCE, December 4, 1879.

A meeting held this evening was called to order at 7¾ o'clock by Vice President Allen.

The Secretary laid before the Society a letter from Col. Thomas Lincoln Casey, U. S. A., of Washington, D. C., and a letter from Mr. Royal Woodward, of Albany, N. Y., the former acknowledging the honor of his election as a corresponding member of the Society, and the latter as a life member, and both expressing a warm interest in the objects of the institution.

The Secretary also laid before the Society a letter from Mr. James Eddy Mauran, of Newport, offering to sell at cost a chest of papers which the owner purchased with the view of their preservation and final transfer to the Historical Cabinet. Some of the papers relate to the purchase of land, buildings and supplies for light-houses; some from David Howell, and others relate to the seizure of vessels from 1798 to 1816; some relate to revenue suits prior to 1800; some are fishery bounty papers; some are books and correspondence relating to the State loan of 1786, among which are letters of the leading capitalists of the State at that time; some relate to divers legal settlements, and all are of an historical character, and have a special interest to Providence. The letter was received and referred to the Librarian to be reported on at the annual meeting.

The Librarian announced the donations received since the last meeting, among which were mound builders' beads, which were taken from a mound in Georgia, and used to belong to a President of the Georgia Historical Society,— presented by a lady.

Rev. Frederick Denison read, by request, the Report of the Committee on the Angell-Johnston Indian Pottery Development. The report was received and ordered on file to be printed with the Proceedings of the Society. The report was then adopted, and Messrs. William G. R. Mowry, Frederick Denison and Henry T. Beckwith were appointed a Committee to carry into action the views contained in the report.

REPORT OF THE COMMITTEE OF THE RHODE ISLAND HISTORICAL SOCIETY ON THE OLD INDIAN STEATITE POTTERY.

Your Committee, after different meetings, visits and examinations of the quarry in Johnston, and consultations with scholars and business men, having duly weighed all evidence and opinions, respectfully report the following facts and recommendations:

I. THE FACTS.

1. This ledge of soapstone is located in Johnston, R. I., about one-eighth of a mile west of the Greek Tavern, north of the Hartford turnpike, on the lands of Mr. Horatio N. Angell.

2. The quarry was first opened by Mr. Angell in February, 1878, from which time it has attracted large and increasing attention both within our State and far beyond it.

3. The stratum of steatite containing the pottery is about twenty-five feet in thickness, having a dip to the east, and has now been cleared of drift and the debris of Indian art for the space of about a hundred feet. It lies between walls of slate stone.

4. In this stratum are several excavations made by the aborigines in securing stone pots, pans, dishes and pipes. One excavation, however, surpasses all others in magnitude and the marks of Indian workmanship.

5. This largest excavation measures about ten feet in length, six feet

in width, and now five feet in depth; but from the top of the ledge, as left by the glaciers, the excavation must have been carried down about fifteen feet or more, inasmuch as when it was opened there lay across its top a fallen slab of slate stone that once stood full ten feet high above it, forming its eastern wall.

6. The excavation was found partly filled with dirt, debris of Indian art, some whole stone pots, some partly finished pots, some only blocked out, numerous stone hammers, the horns of a deer, the bones of an animal and a few shells. Many of these valuable relics have passed into private hands and are highly prized.

7. The sides and bottom of this excavation contain about sixty distinct pits and knobs of places where pots and dishes were cut from the rock, while all parts bear marks and scars made by the stone implements of the swarthy quarrymen.

8. From the excavations and their surroundings have been removed about three hundred horse cart loads of the stone chips left by the Indian workmen, yet some have been preserved by Prof. J. W. P. Jenks, in the Museum of Brown University.

9. Sections of the quarry revealing Indian workmanship and specimens of the workmen's chips have been secured by the Smithsonian Institution, the Permanent Exhibition at Philadelphia, the Museum of Brown University, the Peabody Museum at Cambridge, the Boston Society of Natural History, and the Franklin Society of Providence.

10. Some of the stone pots found in the excavations, amid the debris, are now a part of the very valuable private Indian Cabinet of Mr. Charles Gorton, of this city.

11. Naturalists, ethnologists and students of history are anxious to secure views and specimens from this remarkable quarry. An able report of it was made by Prof. Putnam, Curator of the Peabody Museum.

12. It is a historical fact stated by Hutchinson, (p. 458,) and quoted by Potter in his History of Narragansett, (p. 8,) that the Narragansetts were distinguished for mechanical arts and trade, and furnished earthen vessels and pots for cooking to the adjacent native tribes.

13. It is confidently computed by men of judgment in such premises that this quarry must have been worked by the aborigines for centuries before whites visited this coast, and that, first and last, this ledge must have yielded thousands of pieces of stone ware.

14. So far as now known this ledge is the only pottery of the kind in New England, and must have been exceedingly valuable and famed among all the tribes of the country.

15. All who have visited the pottery have instinctively felt that somehow it ought to be preserved; and those who have studied it most are the most emphatic in this opinion.

16. The conviction of all minds is that it ought to be secured and held as a revelation and monument of Indian life and a historical treasure of Rhode Island.

17. The citizens of Providence and of the State, so far as they have expressed themselves, are unanimous and hearty in their approval of the action taken by the Rhode Island Historical Society, and indicate a readiness to support the Society in any wise and effectual plan for securing and preserving the section of the ledge containing the wonderful workshop.

18. The owner of the ledge is ready and anxious to co-operate with the Society in any proper plan for preserving the unique memorial.

19. Photographic views of the ledge from different positions have been secured by Mr. Angell, and fine stereoscopic views of the excavations were secured by Prof. J. W. P. Jenks, Curator of the Museum of Brown University.

20. This ancient Indian workshop, properly preserved, would be a fitting, perpetual and impressive monument of the life, arts and customs of the aboriginal tribes of Rhode Island, whose hands executed it, and a rare historical and ethnological treasure in our country.

21. It is felt that it might reflect very seriously upon our historical knowledge and our archæological taste and interests, to suffer this ancient and conspicuous evidence of Indian art and workmanship to be broken up or secured by parties out of our State, as we fear it may be.

22. While relics and memorials of old nations are being eagerly sought in all lands at vast expense and treasured in costly museums, as aids in the study of history, archæology, and anthropology — all studies of vital interest — it is urged that Rhode Island cannot afford to be indifferent to the most remarkable memorial of Indian life in New England, providentially found in her own borders, and described in Prof. Putnam's able report of it as of superior worth.

23. So far as we have been able to calculate, after taking counsel of good judges, the large excavation may be secured and eligibly located in our already beautiful Roger Williams Park, to be henceforth carefully protected, at a cost of about six hundred dollars.

In view of these facts, your Committee would report

## II. RECOMMENDATIONS.

1. That a Committee of three be chosen to form and execute a plan for obtaining and preserving the old Indian Steatite Quarry and Pottery as above mentioned, in a section of the ledge to measure about twelve feet in length, nine feet in width and seven feet in depth, or of such size as may seem to be most suitable, provided the citizens of Providence and of the State are willing to contribute the funds necessary for the purpose.

2. That inasmuch as the worthy idea of having, at some time, a museum of Indian art in Roger Williams Park has been entertained and encouraged by our city officials and citizens — unless a more suitable location shall be found, the authorities of the city of Providence be respectfully asked to grant a place for the keeping of the memorial in Roger Williams Park; and that they be requested to designate a spot for this pur-

pose, on a slope within sight, at least, of the statue of the founder of the State.

3. That every member of the Society, and every lover of our State's history, feel himself charged with an obligation to co-operate with and assist the Committee in executing the measure here proposed.

4. That the subscriptions made for carrying out the proposed measure be regarded as due when their amount shall reach the sum of six hundred dollars.

5. That copies of this report be put in type for the use of the members of the Society and the Committee, in soliciting the subscriptions required.

All of which is respectfully submitted,

F. DENISON,
ZACHARIAH ALLEN,
WILLIAM G. R. MOWRY.

Hon. Zachariah Allen then read a carefully prepared essay on the domestic life of the Indians, which contained a great amount of valuable information gleaned from numerous authentic sources. The paper was received with marked expressions of satisfaction.

The table, and the shelves and wall behind the President's seat were covered with Indian relics gathered in Rhode Island, and belonging to the remarkable collection of Mr. Charles Gorton, who was highly complimented by Vice President Allen and called upon to give some explanation of the various utensils before him. Mr. Gorton responded to the call, giving a great amount of valuable information in a brief time.

Prof. J. W. P. Jenks, of Brown University, was next called out and made an instructive address, strongly endorsing the views set forth by the Committee.

Mr. H. N. Angell, the proprietor of the Indian pottery establishment, and Mr. F. Denison each answered the call of the Chairman, speaking in a way to entertain and instruct the audience.

On motion of Mr. William A. Mowry, who prefaced his

resolution with some very complimentary remarks, the thanks of the Society were voted to Messrs. Allen, Gorton, Jenks, Angell and Denison for the rich and varied entertainment of the evening. A copy of Mr. Allen's address was asked for to be printed with the Proceedings of the Society, and the desire was expressed that another evening should be devoted to the history of the Indian.

The meeting was numerously attended and its interest was fully sustained till the close at ten o'clock.

The announcement was made that Hon. William D. Brayton would read the next paper on the Oswego Expedition in which Rhode Island Continental troops performed their last service before the declaration of peace in 1783.

Adjourned.

AMOS PERRY, Sec'y.

## SPECIAL MEETING.

PROVIDENCE, December 16, 1879.

A meeting held this evening was called to order at 7¾ o'clock by Vice President Allen.

The Secretary laid before the Society a request signed by Mr. George Edward Allen for the loan of the plat of Camp Sprague to be hung in the Infantry Armory at a meeting to be held on the 30th instant. On motion of Mr. A.V. Jenks, it was

*Voted*, That the Librarian be authorized to grant the request on the usual conditions.

The Librarian announced numerous donations received since the last meeting.

Mr. William G. R. Mowry called attention to a marble block that used to stand at one end of Washington Bridge, and served for many years as a pedestal to the bust of Washington.

Hon. William D. Brayton was then introduced and read a paper on the Oswego Expedition of 1783. He was led to essay a sketch of this military enterprise by a crude ballad which he heard sung in his younger days by a negro familiarly called Prince Greene, who was in the expedition and was made a cripple for life by exposures to biting frosts and by the want of suitable food. The plan of the expedition was explained by means of the correspondence between Washington and Colonel Willet of New York, who was entrusted with the command. The fort at Oswego was to be taken by surprise or not attempted. The effort resulted disastrously. The sketch, which was drawn largely from the authentic documents of the time, closed with the ballad of Prince Greene, which, after pertinent comments and explanations, was admirably read.

The meeting was fully attended and the interest was sustained to the close.

On motion of Rev. E. M. Stone, the thanks of the Society were tendered to Hon. William D. Brayton for his entertaining and valuable paper, a copy of which was requested for the archives of the Society.

Adjourned.

AMOS PERRY, *Sec'y.*

## SPECIAL MEETING.

Providence, December 31, 1879.

A meeting was held this evening beginning at a quarter before eight o'clock, Vice President Allen in the chair.

The record of the last meeting was read and approved.

William B. Weeden, Esq., was then introduced and read an historical sketch of the rise of person and property, illustrating his subject by numerous references and quotations. The paper was the result of learning, research and industry, and showed conclusively that person and property have advanced together in the progress of the world.

At the conclusion of the reading, Prof. J. L. Lincoln highly complimented the learning and research of the lecturer, and moved the following resolution :

*Resolved*, That the thanks of the Society be presented to William B. Weeden, Esq., for his scholarly, interesting and instructive paper, and that a copy of the same be requested for the archives of the Society.

The motion was seconded by Isaac H. Southwick, Esq., and after some pithy remarks by Vice President Allen, was unanimously passed.

Despite a severe storm of snow and sleet, about thirty of our prominent business men were in attendance and listened attentively to the discussion of a subject intimately connected with their affairs. The interest of the meeting was fully sustained, though the Chairman expressed his fears at the outset lest the absence of ladies might have a depressing effect.

After notice that the annual meeting would be held on the 13th of January the meeting was, on motion, adjourned.

Amos Perry, *Sec'y.*

## ANNUAL MEETING.

Providence, January 13, 1880.

The annual meeting was held this evening at 7½ o'clock, Vice President Allen in the chair.

The Secretary read the records of the last special meeting and of the last annual meeting; also a letter from Hon. Francis Brinley, of Newport, expressing regret at his inability to be present, and his warm interest in the objects of the Society.

The Treasurer read his annual report, showing the Society to be in a better financial condition than ever before. He also presented a supplemental report containing a statement of numerous facts, both interesting and encouraging to the members of the Society.

The Librarian and Cabinet Keeper laid before the Society his annual report, showing that the last year has been one of marked progress, and appealing for earnest effort to supply manifest needs.

The report of Mr. George C. Mason as Procurator for Newport county was read by the Secretary. It urged earnest and systematic efforts to secure biographical sketches of distinguished deceased citizens of the State, and a copy of Dr. Ezra Styles' diary kept at Newport during the time of the Revolutionary War.

The Secretary also read the report of Mr. William J. Miller, as Procurator for Bristol county, who spoke of the proposed monument to Massasoit, at Warren, and of the bi-centennial celebration that is to take place at Bristol.

The Committee on Nomination of New Members, recommended the following named gentlemen for membership, and they were accordingly elected:

RESIDENT MEMBERS.—James Coates, Christopher Lippitt, William D. Brayton, Augustine Jones, E. Webster Clarke, William H Chandler, Marsden J. Perry, George A. Seagraves, Daniel Burrows, Charles L. Potter, Providence; Samuel Clarke, Lincoln; Albert C. Howard, East Providence; Wilfred H. Munroe, Bristol; Amos G. Nichols, Hopkinton; William R. Sayles, Pawtucket.

CORRESPONDING MEMBERS.—Prof. Moses Coit Tyler, Ann Arbor, Michigan; Samuel Dunster, Esq., Attleboro' Falls, Mass.

HONORARY MEMBER.—Hon. Carl Schurz, Washington, D. C.

The report of the Committee on Grounds and Building was read by Mr. Southwick, showing a detailed account of the expenses incurred.

The report of the Committee on Genealogical Researches was read by Mr. William A. Mowry, and contained an encouraging statement in regard to progress in this department of study. On motion of Mr. Mowry, in behalf of the Committee, the following resolution was unanimously passed:

*Resolved*, That the thanks of this Society are hereby given to Dr. Edwin M. Snow and Sidney S. Rider, Esq., for the benefit conferred by them upon the public by their valuable and creditable contribution to the historical literature of Rhode Island in their recent publication of the Registration of Births, Marriages and Deaths of the town and city of Providence.

Rev. E. M. Stone presented a report in behalf of the Committee on Publications, urging the importance and the expediency of issuing a seventh volume of the Society's Proceedings, and this recommendation was endorsed by Vice President Allen.

The foregoing reports were respectively accepted and referred to the Committee on Publications.

Here the Society proceeded to the election of officers for the ensuing year with the following result:

## OFFICERS.

| | | |
|---|---|---|
| President, | Samuel G. Arnold, | Portsmouth. |
| Vice Presidents, | Zachariah Allen, | Providence. |
| | Francis Brinley, | Newport. |
| Secretary, | Amos Perry, | Providence. |
| Treasurer, | Richmond P. Everett, | " |
| Librarian and Cabinet Keeper, | Edwin M Stone, | " |
| Committee on Nomination of New Members, | Albert V. Jenks, | " |
| | William Staples, | " |
| | W. Maxwell Greene, | " |
| Committee on Lectures and Reading of Papers, | William Gammell, | " |
| | Charles W. Parsons, | " |
| | Amos Perry, | " |
| Committee on Publications of the Society, | John R. Bartlett, | " |
| | J. Lewis Diman, | " |
| | Edwin M. Stone, | " |
| Committee on Genealogical Researches, | Henry E. Turner, | Newport. |
| | William A. Mowry, | Providence. |
| | Bennett J. Munro, | Bristol |
| Committee on Care of Grounds and Building, | Isaac H. Southwick, | Providence. |
| | Henry J. Steere, | " |
| | Royal C. Taft, | " |
| Audit Committee, | Henry T. Beckwith, | " |
| | Walter Blodget, | " |
| | John P. Walker, | " |
| Procurators, | George C. Mason, | Newport. |
| | William J. Miller, | Bristol. |
| | Erastus Richardson, | Woonsocket. |
| | Henry F. Smith, | Pawtucket. |
| | Charles H. Fisher, | Scituate. |
| | George H. Olney, | Hopkinton. |

A proposed amendment to the Constitution, on which action was postponed at the July quarterly meeting in 1879, was called up, and after some discussion, the question whether the Society should have a Standing Committee on Library, and what should be the duties of said Committee, was referred to a Committee consisting of Mr. William A. Mowry, Prof. J. Lewis Diman and Gen. Horatio Rogers, who were instructed to report at the next quarterly meeting.

The report of the Committee on the State Appropriation was read by Judge Stiness, and gave an account of the progress in cataloguing the Society's works.

The report was received and Messrs. Stiness, Parsons and Weeden were appointed to fulfill the duties of the said Committee till the establishment of a Library Committee.

Vice President Allen reported verbally in behalf of the Committee on the Slate Rock Monument. The report was accepted and the same Committee, consisting of Messrs. Allen, Diman and Walker, was continued.

The Committee on the Indian Pottery Development reported progress.

On motion of Mr. J. P. Walker, it was

*Voted,* That the Committee on Publications be authorized to have printed five hundred copies of the Reports of the Society, with the Proceedings and Necrology of 1879-80, the expense of the same not to exceed one hundred and seventy-five dollars.

On motion of Mr. J. A. Howland it was

*Voted,* That a tax of three dollars be assessed on each resident member to defray the current expenses of the year.

Rev. E. M. Stone made a verbal report in regard to certain historical documents that are offered to the Society by Mr. James E. Mauran, of Newport. The Committee considered the documents valuable, and offered to contribute one-quarter of the forty dollars required for their purchase.

The Secretary tendered his resignation, but the Society promptly adjourned without taking action thereon.

AMOS PERRY, *Sec'y.*

# REPORTS OF OFFICERS AND COMMITTEES

PRESENTED TO THE

ANNUAL MEETING, JANUARY 13, 1880.

AND

# NECROLOGY, 1879-80.

# TREASURER'S REPORTS.

*Dr.    Richmond P. Everett, Treasurer, in account with the Rhode Island
            Historical Society.*
1879.
Jan. 14.   To cash on hand,   -   -   -   -   $718 26
           Interest from Life Membership Account in Providence
              Institution for Savings,   -   -   -   11 80
Dec. 17.   Interest from Life Membership Account in Providence
              Institution for Savings,   -   -   -   13 00
1880.
Jan. 13.   Taxes from 163 members at $3,   -   -   489 00
           Admission fees from 17 members at $5,   -   -   85 00
           Subscriptions for arranging and work in Library
              from members, as follows:—
                 Henry J. Steere,   -   -   $50 00
                 Henry T. Beckwith,   -   -   50 00
                 William Greene,   -   -   50 00
                 Rowland Hazard,   -   -   -   50 00
                 H. Conant,   -   -   -   25 00
                                              ———
                                              225 00
           For sale of books and pamphlets,   -   -   -   27 35
           Subscriptions for printing Reports of 1878–79,   -   36 72
                                              ————
                                              $1,606 13

*Cr.    Richmond P. Everett, Treasurer, in account with the Rhode Island
            Historical Society.*
1879.
Jan. 22.   Providence Press Co., for printing Reports of 1877–8,   $243 98
              Amount carried forward,   -   -   -   $243 98

|  |  |  |  |
|---|---|---|---|
|  | Brought forward, | | $243 98 |
| July 21. | Treasurer, for amount advanced by him in 1878, | | 312 25 |
| 1880. | | | |
| Jan. 13. | Providence Press Co., for printing Reports, 1878-9, | | 186 72 |
|  | Printing, advertising meetings, expresses and postages, | | 165 74 |
|  | Fuel, gas and janitor, | | 150 29 |
|  | Library Committee, | | 95 15 |
|  | Building and grounds, | | 85 53 |
|  | Sewer tax, | | 100 35 |
|  | Magazines and books, | | 15 60 |
|  | Balance on hand, | | 250 52 |
|  | | | $1,606 13 |
|  | There is on deposit in the Providence Institution for Savings, | | $243 26 |
|  | Treasurer, | | 7 26 |
|  | | | $250 52 |

RICHMOND P. EVERETT, *Treasurer.*

PROVIDENCE, January 13, 1880.

The undersigned have examined the above report, and compared same with vouchers, and find it correct.

HENRY T. BECKWITH,
WALTER BLODGET,
JOHN P. WALKER,
*Audit Committee.*


## LIFE MEMBERSHIP ACCOUNT.

*Dr.* Richmond P. Everett, Treasurer, in account with the Rhode Island Historical Society.

|  |  |  |  |
|---|---|---|---|
| 1879. | | | |
| Jan. 14. | To cash on hand, | | $599 82 |
|  | Life membership of Samuel G. Arnold, | | 50 00 |
|  | Interest from Providence Institution for Savings, | | 11 98 |
| July 8. | Life membership of Amos D. Lockwood, | | 50 00 |
| 16. | Interest from Providence Institution for Savings, | | 13 00 |
| Oct. 16. | Life membership of Royal Woodward, of Albany, N. Y., | | 50 00 |
| 1880. | | | |
| Jan. 7. | Life membership of Charles Gorton, | | 50 00 |
|  | | | $824 80 |

TREASURER'S REPORT. 51

Cr.  Richmond P. Everett, Treasurer, in account with the Rhode Island
Historical Society.

1879.
March 26. Interest from Providence Institution for Savings,      $11 80
Dec.  27.     "        "         "           "          "        13 00
1880.
Jan.  13. Balance on hand,      -     -     -     -             800 00
                                                               ───────
                                                                $824 80

There is on deposit in the Providence Institution
for Savings,      -       -       -       $800 00

RICHMOND P. EVERETT, *Treasurer.*

PROVIDENCE, January 13, 1880.

The undersigned have examined the above report, and compared it with the vouchers, and find the same correct.

HENRY T. BECKWITH,
WALTER BLODGET,
JOHN P. WALKER,
*Audit Committee.*

# REPORT OF THE NORTHERN DEPARTMENT

OF THE

# RHODE ISLAND HISTORICAL SOCIETY.

This fifty-eighth annual meeting finds the Rhode Island Historical Society in a healthful condition. Its various committees have been prompt in the discharge of their respective duties. The Librarian, besides answering numerous letters of inquiry addressed to him from various parts of the country, and aiding inquiries of a local character, has devoted much time to soliciting and obtaining contributions to its collections. Under the direction of a special committee, Mrs. Rebecca R. Cushing, has continued the work of cataloguing the Society's collections and of examining our files of newspapers for the purpose of ascertaining their deficiencies. This latter has been completed. Our newspapers are among the most valuable of our treasures, affording, as they do, a rich mine of facts for the historian, the biographer, and genealogist.

### PAPERS READ.

The papers read before the Society were eleven in number, as follows:

1879.

January 28. Hon. Abraham Payne, on The Life and Times of Jonathan Edwards.

February 11. Col. John Ward, of New York, on The Siege of Harper's Ferry by Stonewall Jackson.

February 25. Dr. Henry E. Turner, of Newport, on Jeremiah Clarke and his descendants.

March 11. John Austin Stevens, Esq., of New York, on The French in Rhode Island.

May 20. Rev. George E. Ellis, D. D., of Boston, on The Present Indian Question with our Government.

October 10. Hon. Isaac N. Arnold, of Chicago, on The Northern Campaign of 1777, including the Military Services of General Benedict Arnold.

November 5. General Horatio Rogers, on La Corne St. Luc, the leader of Burgoyne's Indians.

November 19. Professor J. L. Lincoln, on The Character and Works of the Historian Tacitus.

December 4. Rev. Frederick Denison read by request a Report of the Committee on the Angell-Johnston-Indian-Pottery Development.

December 16. Hon. William D. Brayton, on The Oswego Expedition of 1783.

December 21. William B. Weeden, Esq., on The Rise of Person and Property.

### CONTRIBUTIONS.

The contributions for the year number 3,025. Of these, 2,440 were pamphlets; 331 bound volumes of books; 50 unbound volumes of books; 14 bound and 18 unbound volumes of newspapers; 48 manuscripts; and 23 maps, plats and charts. The residue comprise engravings, broadsides, hand-bills, single newspapers, cuttings, and articles of *virtu*.

Among the books specially noticeable are the valuable scientific works issued by the Federal Government, that come to us through the State, Treasury, War, Navy and Interior Departments, and the Smithsonian Institution. Besides being fine specimens of the printer's art, many of them are profusely illustrated with prints as pleasing to the eye as the text is instructive to the mind.

By exchanges and a few purchases a considerable number of town histories have been added to our collections. One of our valuable acquisitions is "The Genealogies and Estates in Charlestown, Mass.," in two volumes, — a work of immense painstaking. This work, comprising eleven hundred and seventy-eight pages, was commenced and advanced by Thomas Bellows Wyman, an earnest antiquary, but whose lamented death, in 1878, prevented its completion by his hand. In accordance with his expressed will, the labor of finishing the work was assigned to Rev. Henry H. Edes, to whose industry, care and fidelity, every page bears honorable testimony. To persons seeking to trace their connections with the early settlers of Charlestown these volumes will be found of great value.

One of the latest Genealogies, worthy of special notice, is that of "The Whitney Family of Connecticut" and its affiliations, representing the descendants of Henry Whitney, 1649 to 1878, by Stephen Whitney Phœnix, Esq., of New York. It was completed in 1879, and is comprised in three volumes (quarto) of 2,740 pages, being the largest privately printed work of the kind ever issued in Europe or America. The edition consists of ten folio and five hundred quarto copies, all for presentation — one of which is in the library of the Rhode Island Historical Society. The work is worthy of careful inspection by every one interested in the study of genealogy, for its merits cannot be fully described. Ten years of constant labor were devoted to it by Mr. Phœnix, and he wrote upwards of fourteen thousand letters, to many of which no replies were received — so little interest do some people take in the preservation of family history. Several years ago the last revised proofs were returned to the printer with the manuscript, and twenty minutes later both the manuscript and the text of the whole work were destroyed by fire in the city of New York. *Phœnix* like he recommenced his genealogy on a more extensive scale than before, seeking new materials; and the commendable result achieved is the enviable reward of his patient toil and persevering industry. That it was a labor of love is obvious from the inscription it bears: "I inscribe these volumes to the dear memory of my beloved mother, Mary, daughter of Stephen and Harriet Whitney, for whose tender love and devotion I owe a debt of more than filial gratitude and reverence." The volumes contain particulars of twenty thousand three hundred and sixty one principal persons, whose names are in heavy-faced type, and there are admirable indexes of places and surnames, which are invaluable.[*]

In 1867, a genealogy of The Descendants of John Phœnix, an early settler of Kittery, Maine, was privately printed by the Bradstreet Press for Mr. Phœnix, and he has ready for publication the Genealogy of the Family of Alexander Phœnix, the first emigrant, born in England in 1613.

---

[*] Next to the Whitney Genealogy in point of magnitude is that of the Taylor Family of England.

Mr. Phœnix has also given much personal attention to the neglected portraits of American worthies in *Old New York*, many of which he has had engraved, from time to time, and distributed to friends. The Records of the Reformed (Dutch) Church since 1639, and of the First Presbyterian Church in New York, have been carefully copied and are being printed in the New York Genealogical and Biographical Record, solely at his request, by which many persons will be enabled hereafter to trace their ancestors and write up their genealogies.

From Samuel Dunster, Esq., of 'South Attleboro', Mass., we have received the "Genealogy of the Dunster Family," a work of thorough research, and an important contribution to that department of literature.

To Joseph J. Cooke, Esq., of Providence, we are indebted for a copy of the "Genealogy of the Russell Family," edited by Hon. John R. Bartlett. Besides a full account of the Russells, and collateral branches of the family, and of the Drowne family, prepared by Henry T. Drowne, Esq., of New York, the value of the volume is enhanced by a comprehensive notice, written by Albert R. Cooke, Esq., of Governor Nicholas Cooke, one of the eminent Rhode Island patriots of the Revolution, whose life and services deserve commemoration in an independent biography. Mr. Bartlett brought to his work the spirit of a true genealogist, and has completed his task with commendable skill.

Another work of this class which we are glad to have on our shelves, is the "Genealogy of the Tilley Family," compiled by Mr. R. Hammitt Tilley, of Newport. In this brochure of seventy-nine pages, Mr. Tilley has brought together the results of extensive investigation, and deservedly takes rank with writers of this class. Mr. Tilley is still pursuing his investigations, with a view to issuing a second and more complete edition of his family record.

Claudius B. Farnsworth, Esq., of Pawtucket, R. I., has thoughtfully placed in our library, "Epitaphs from the Old Burying Ground in Groton, Mass.," with Notes and Appendix; a handsomely printed volume of two hundred and seventy-one pages, prepared by Samuel A. Green, M. D., with his well known accuracy, making a valuable contribution to mortuary literature.

Still another genealogical work of importance, presented to our Society by its author, Mr. Charles Henry James Douglas, is "A Collection of Family Records with Biographical Sketches and other Memoranda of

Families and Individuals bearing the name of Douglas." This volume of five hundred and sixty-three pages contains the Douglas Coat of Arms and twelve portraits. The work was pursued and completed while the author was a student in Brown University, at which he was graduated in 1879.

From the Royal Historical Society of Great Britain, has been received Volume VIII. of its Transactions, recently published, edited by its learned Secretary, Rev. Charles Rogers, LL. D. It consists of sixteen independent papers, among them Notes on the Study of History, by the Editor; Domestic Every Day Life, Manners and Customs in England from the earliest period to the end of the eighteenth century, etc.; Early Laws and Customs in Great Britain Regarding Food; Alexander in Afghanistan; and much other matter interesting alike to the antiquary and to the popular reader. The work is a valuable acquisition to any library.

The learned Societies with which we are in correspondence, at home and abroad, have continued, as heretofore, their acceptable contributions to our collections, while a number of individuals, like Dr. Samuel A. Green, of Boston, and Henry Thayer Drowne, Esq., of New York, have not failed to show a substantial interest in the objects of our Society. To the Smithsonian Institution we are still under obligations for courtesies in facilitating foreign exchanges, as we also are for its valued publications. To the National Bureau of Education, to General A. A. Humphreys, Hon. John Jay Knox, and to the Departments of State, of the Treasury, of the Interior, of the Navy, and of War, thanks are due and tendered, for valuable publications issued from the government press.

A silver watch presented to the Society by Mrs. Louisa Lippitt Herlitz, worn by her husband, the late Captain Joseph Herlitz, when the vessel he commanded (the ship Ganges) was, by the force of the terrific gale of September 22d and 23d, 1815, wrecked against the Washington Building, in this city, is an interesting souvenir of an event which raised the tide more than seven feet higher than ever before known, submerged a large portion of the business part of the town, carried away the great bridge, drove between thirty and forty vessels into the cove, spread devastation in every direction, and forced the ocean spray forty miles into the country. Captain Herlitz was an enterprising ship master, highly esteemed, and the watch here named, made by Richard Farrell, of Dublin, Ireland, was a gift to him from the owners of the vessel of which he was in command, as a token of their confidence and respect. He died in Providence, December 20th, 1819, in the thirty-fifth year of his age, and was buried with Masonic honors.

A reminder of the building of Washington Bridge has been added to our collections in the form of a marble tablet, bearing the following inscription:

WASHINGTON BRIDGE.

Built by

JOHN BROWN, Esq. 1793.

This MONUMENT is erected by the Founder and Proprietor
of India Point, As a Testimony of High
Respect for the
GREAT & ILLUSTRIOUS WASHINGTON.

The monument here mentioned, of the base of which the tablet was a part, was a life-size statue of Washington, carved in wood, by John Bowers, of Providence, and erected at the west end of the bridge. It was swept away and lost in the great September gale already spoken of. The building of this bridge was connected in the mind of Mr. Brown with the extension of his commercial pursuits. He was a man of great enterprise, and at this time a leading merchant, having twenty sail of ships engaged in commerce. He took a prominent part in the affairs of town and State, during the Revolution, was one of the celebrated company which, in 1772, burned the Gaspee, as the first outbreak of a resistance to the mother country in Rhode Island, and in 1784, was chosen to represent his native State in Congress, a position to which he was repeatedly re-elected. In carrying out his business plans, Mr. Brown filled in about four acres of the flats near the western terminus of the bridge, and established a wharf flush with deep water. He also built a ship of one thousand tons burthen, which he named the Washington, the largest vessel, at that time, that had ever been built in America, designed for the India trade,—a trade then highly lucrative. The cost was $300,000. Freighted with a suitable cargo, she sailed for China, where, without consulting the owner, and to his painful regret, she was sold by the supercargo. By this unexpected transaction, Mr. Brown's high hopes were swept away, and commerce at India Point dwindled. Mr. Brown was born in Providence, January 27th, 1736, and died September 20th, 1803, in the sixty-eighth year of his age. On his tomb stone, beneath his name, is inscribed:

"The enterprising and accomplished Merchant,
The tried Patriot and wise Legislator,
The universal Philanthropist and sincere Christian."

For this interesting relic of eighty-seven years gone by the Society is indebted to Mr. Benjamin J. Brown, now in the eighty-third year of his age.

OUR CONTRIBUTORS.

Exclusive of thirty-six volumes of history and biography, and nine pamphlets, obtained in exchange for duplicate publications, the contributions to the Society's collections before enumerated have been received from the following societies and individuals:

Maine Historical Society,
Massachusetts Historical Society,
American Antiquarian Society,
Essex Institute,
N. E. Historical and Genealogical Register,
Worcester Society of Antiquity,
Massachusetts State Library,
Boston Public Library,
State of Massachusetts,
New Hampshire Historical Society,
Old Colony Historical Society,
Vermont Historical Society,
Vermont State Library,
Connecticut Historical Society,
New Haven Historical Society,
Yale College Library,
New York Historical Society,
New York American News Co.,
New York Mercantile Library,
New York State Library,
Philadelphia Library Co.,
Long Island Historical Society,
Minnesota Historical Society,
New Jersey Historical Society,
Orange (N. J.) New England Society,
Oneida Historical Society,
Pennsylvania Historical Society,
American Philosophical Society,
Delaware Historical Society,
Chicago Historical Society,
Congressional Library, Washington,
Department of State, Washington,
Department of Engineers, Washington,
Department of War, Washington,
Department of the Interior, Washington,
Department of Agriculture, Washington,
Department of the Treasury, Washington,
Bureau of Education, Washington,
Smithsonian Institution, Washington,
Ohio Historical Society,
Cleveland Historical Society,
Wisconsin Historical Society,
R. I. Soldiers and Sailors' Historical Society,
Iowa Historical Society,
Minnesota Historical Society,
Minnesota Academy of Natural Sciences,
Chicago Historical Society,
Maryland Historical Society,
Montana Historical Society,

## REPORT OF NORTHERN DEPARTMENT. 59

Virginia Historical Society,
Southern Historical Society,
Georgia Historical Society,
South Carolina Historical Society,
Kentucky Historical Society,
Quebec Historical Society,
Massachusetts Railroad Commissioners,
Royal University, Christiania, Norway,
Royal Society Northern Antiquaries, Copenhagen, Denmark,
Royal Historical Society, London,
Royal Society Arts and Sciences. Lisbon, Portugal.
Halifax Historical Society,
Institution Ethnologique, Paris,
State of Rhode Island,
City of Providence,
Rhode Island State Board of Charities,
Rhode Island Medical Society,
William A. Mowry, Providence,
Rhode Island Hospital, "
Hon. John R. Bartlett, "
Richmond P. Everett, "
H. M. Coombs & Co., "
Albert V. Jenks, "
Joseph J. Cooke, "
Rt. Rev. Thomas M. Clark, Providence,
Hon. Thomas A. Doyle, Providence,
Rev. Edwin M. Stone, "
John S. Ormsbee, "
James P. Walker, "
Mrs. J. B. Hoskins, "
Mrs. Louisa Lippitt Herlitz, "
Samuel Green, "
Stephen D Greene, "

Miss P. Jackson, Providence,
Albert T. Elliott, "
Frank M. Burrough, "
Eben E. Thaxter, "
Mrs. John Carter Brown, "
William Viall, "
Christopher Burr, "
Hon. Joshua M. Addeman, "
Hon. John H. Stiness, "
Hon. Amos Perry, "
Edwin Barrows, "
George W. Davis, "
Mrs. George Richmond, "
Sidney S. Rider, "
John A. Howland, "
George T. Paine, "
Asa M. Gammell, "
Mrs. William Earle, "
Gen. Horatio Rogers, "
Rev. N. Williams, "
Charles W. Parsons, M. D., "
Henry T. Beckwith, "
William A. Harris, "
Rev. Carlton A. Staples, "
Rev. Samuel H. Webb, "
William E. Brown, "
Rev. Thomas Laurie, D. D., "
Rev. Frederic Denison, "
J. A. & R. A. Reid, "
Reuben A. Guild, LL. D., "
J. V. C. Joslin, "
Hon. Samuel G. Arnold, Portsmouth, R. I ,
George C. Mason, Esq., Newport,
William J. Miller, Esq , Bristol, R. I.,
J. G. Perry, South Kingstown, R. I ,
C. B. Farnsworth, Pawtucket,
Prof. Joseph Eastman, East Greenwich,

Sam W. Clarke, Warwick, R. I.,
Hon. Marshal P. Wilder, Boston, Mass.,
Samuel A. Green, M. D., Boston, Mass.,
George B. Reed, Boston, Mass.,
Hon. Richard Frothingham, Boston, Mass.,
Charles F. Folsom, M. D., Boston, Mass.,
Sampson, Davenport & Co., Boston, Mass.,
Alexander Williams, Boston, Mass.,
Hon. Alfred Turner, " "
A. M. Knapp, " "
Hon. Robert C. Winthrop, Boston, Mass.,
Rev. Robert C. Waterston, Boston, Mass.,
Phineas Bates, Jr., Esq., Boston, Mass.,
Houghton & Co , Boston, Mass.,
Rev. P. D. Peet, Clinton, Wisconsin,
Hon. Charles Deane, Cambridge, Mass.,
Rev. Elmer M. Capen, D. D., Somerville, Mass.,
James S. Pike, New York,
Hon Henry K. Oliver, Salem, Mass.,
Iowa *Churchman*,
Frederick Muller, Amsterdam,
Rev. William Hague, D. D.,
Hon. Mark Kimball, Chicago,
A. S. Gatschet, Washington,
J. Austin Stevens, New York,
H. H. Morgan, St. Louis,
Gen. A. A. Humphreys, Washington, D. C.
Benjamin Perley Poore, Esq , Washington, D. C.,
J. A. Farwell, Chicago, Ill.,
Lippincott & Co , Philadelphia,
J. W. Bouton, New York,
Rev. Arthur C. Stilson, Ottumwa, Iowa,
R. A. Brock, Esq., Richmond, Va.,
Col. Charles C. Jones, Jr., Augusta, Ga.,
Col. John Ward, New York,
J. Fletcher Williams, St. Paul, Minn.,
Rev. T. S. Drowne, D. D., Garden City, Long Island, N. Y.,
Henry Thayer Drowne, New York,
Prof. Asa Bird Gardner, West Point,
Gov. Hartranft, Harrisburg, Pa.,
James B. Angell, LL. D., Ann Arbor, Mich.,
Franklin A. Dexter, Esq., New Haven, Ct.,
Rev. Samuel Osgood, D. D., New York,
B. F. Stevens, London,
Frederick A. Holden, Washington,
Hon. John J. Knox. "
Hon. James A. Garfield, "
Hon. C. C. Patterson, "
Hon. John Eaton, "
Hon. Henry B. Anthony, "
H. W. Howgate, "
Hon. A. E. Burnside, "
Hon William G. Ledru, "
Hon. Benjamin T. Eames, "
Hon D. M. Key, "
E. Dufossé, Paris.
Alexander Duncan, Esq., England,
Anonymous,

Editors of *Tuftonian*, Somerville, Mass.,
Barnes & Co., New York,
Henry E. Turner, M. D., Newport, R. I.,
Benjamin Rhodes, Newport, R. I.,
Ferree & Co, Philadelphia,
Rev. James M. Hoppin, D. D., New Haven, Ct.,
Rev. J. H. Mellish, South Scituate, R. I.,
Mrs. Jane A. Eames, Concord, N. H.,
American Unitarian Association, Boston, Mass.,
Frederic W. Lincoln, Boston, Mass.
Hon. Charles Francis Adams, Cambridge, Mass.,
George H Greene, Lansing, Mich.,
Henry Phillips, Jr., Ph. D., Philadelphia,
Alfred E. Whittaker, San Francisco, Cal.,
James S. Pike,
M. D. Gilman, Montpelier, Vt.,
Samuel A. Dunster, South Attleboro, Mass.,
William W. Wheldon, Concord, Mass.,
George Washington Warren, Boston, Mass.,

## A HUNDRED YEARS AGO.

The year just closed and the year upon which we have now entered furnish striking contrasts in the condition of Rhode Island to-day with its condition a century ago. Then, the population of the State numbered not more than 52,000;* now, assuming that the increase from 1875 to 1880 has equalled that shown during the period from 1870 to 1875, the population of the State is about 275,000. Then, the population of Providence did not exceed 4,000; now, it exhibits over 104,000. Then, our sister capital, Newport, numbered about 5,000 souls; now, more than 15,000. Then, the State was oppressed with the burthen of war, and in the struggle for national life, giving to the country the service of its entire male population between the ages of sixteen and sixty; Newport and Providence were occupied as military camps and hospitals, and the entire sea line of Rhode Island required constant guarding against the invasion of an enemy watching opportunities from its central position at New York; now, the arts of peace are smiling upon the people, and filling them with a joyousness in those days of peril unknown, the music of a prosperous industry in the various departments of agriculture, commerce, manufactures and mechanic arts is everywhere heard; horse-back mail carrying, and slow-coach

---

*According to the census of 1782 the population of the State was 52,347; the population of Providence was then 4,310; and of Newport, 5,530.

passenger conveyance have given place to railroad and steamboat transit; while education, in its elementary and higher departments, in obedience to the demand of a healthful public sentiment, is freely shedding its blessings upon every one of every class, willing to accept them. Then, to visit Boston from Providence was a wearisome day's ride; now, that visit may be made in seventy-five minutes! Then, the people were content to hear from foreign lands once in forty days or three months; now, we open the morning papers and read the doings of the previous day in England, continental Europe, Turkey, Egypt, Afghanistan and China! What still greater wonders, in the way of progress, the phonograph, the telephone, and other developments of science, have in store for us, it would be vain to even conjecture.

### AN EARLY PROCLAMATION.

But while a hundred years ago the people of Rhode Island were sorely pressed by the calamities of war, they were not unmindful of the justice of their cause, nor doubtful of an ultimate successful result. They believed in a superintending Providence as a power that shaped the destinies of nations as of individuals, and to whom it was but the prompting of reverential trust to look for direction in all seasons of trial, and for aid in threatening exigencies. It was in this view that Governor William Greene, a true son of Rhode Island, and a patriot of the noblest type, issued the following proclamation, which is here reproduced as a specimen of the spirit by which himself and the leading minds of the State were actuated while stimulating the people to persistent resistance of oppression, and a vindication of their civil rights.

*Proclamation for Fast.*

By His Excellency, WILLIAM GREENE, Esq.,

Governor, Captain General, and Commander-in-Chief of and over the State of Rhode Island and Providence Plantations:

### A PROCLAMATION.

WHEREAS the Most Honorable the Congress of the United States of America did, on the Eleventh Day of March last, pass the following Resolve, to wit:

"It having pleased the righteous Governor of the World, for the Punishment of our manifold Offences, to permit the Sword of War still to harrass our Country, it becomes us to endeavor, by humbling ourselves before him, and turning from every evil Way, to avert his Anger, and obtain his Favor and Blessing: It is therefore hereby recommended to the several States,

"That WEDNESDAY, the 26th day of April next, be set apart and observed as a day of FASTING, HUMILIATION and PRAYER, that we may with one Heart and one Voice implore the Sovereign Lord of Heaven and Earth to remember Mercy in his Judgments;—to make us sincerely penitent for our Transgressions:—to prepare us for Deliverance, and to remove the Evils with which he has been pleased to visit us;—to banish Vice and Irreligion from among us, and establish Virtue and Piety by his Divine Grace;—to bless all public Councils throughout the United States, giving them Wisdom, Firmness and Unanimity, and directing them to the best Measures for the public Good;—to bless the Magistrates and People of every Rank, and animate and unite the Hearts of all to promote the Interest of their Country;—to bless the public Defence, inspiring all Commanders and Soldiers with Magnanimity and Perseverance, and giving Vigor and Success to the Military Operations by Sea and Land;—to bless the illustrious Sovereign and the Nation in Alliance with these States, and all who interest themselves in the Support of our Rights and Liberties;—to make that Alliance of perpetual and extensive Usefulness to those immediately concerned, and Mankind in general; to grant fruitful Seasons and to bless our Industry, Trade and Manufactures;—to bless all Schools and Seminaries of Learning, and every Means of Instruction and Education; to cause Wars to cease, and to establish Peace among the Nations.

"And it is further recommended that servile Labor and Recreation be forbidden on said Day."

And whereas the Council of War appointed to act in the Recess of the General Assembly of the State, taking the aforesaid Resolves into consideration, did on this Day request me to issue a Proclamation to make known the same, and recommending the said Day to be observed accordingly; and that all servile Labor and Recreation be abstained from thereon: I have therefore thought fit to issue this Proclamation, to make known the same, and do hereby recommend it to all the Inhabitants of this State to observe the said Day as a Day of Fasting, Humiliation and Prayer, according to the Intent of said Resolve; and to abstain from all servile Labor and Recreation on that Day.

Given under my Hand and the Seal of the said State, this Eighth Day of April, in the Year of our Lord One Thousand Seven Hundred and Eighty, and in the Fourth Year of Independence.

WILLIAM GREENE.

By His Excellency's Command
    HENRY WARD, Sec'ry.

God save the United States of America.

### INDEPENDENCE IN PROVIDENCE.

Tracing the path of time backward for a little more than half a century we come upon the first commemoration, in Providence, of American Independence. It was a season of universal exultation, and joy found expression in every class of citizens. How could it be otherwise in the home of Stephen Hopkins, Nicholas Cooke, Arthur Fenner, Theodore Foster, Simeon Thayer, Solomon Drowne, Jeremiah Olney, the Browns, the Nightingales, the Bowens, Cyprian Sterry, Joseph Russell, John Mathewson, Silas Downer, Ambrose Page, and others of that ilk?

The Declaration of Independence was received in Providence from Congress on Friday, July 12th, and published in the Providence *Gazette* the following day. Thursday, the 25th of July, was chosen for giving vent to popular feeling. In the meantime the necessary preparations were made, and at eleven o'clock on the morning of that day Governor Cooke, attended by such members of both Houses of Assembly as were in town, together with a number of prominent citizens, went in procession to the State House, escorted by the Cadets and Light Infantry companies, where, at twelve o'clock, was read the Act of Assembly concurring with the General Congress in their Declaration of Independence. The Declaration was also read by George Brown, then upwards of eighty years old. He was selected on account of the compass of his voice, and so firm and clear was his utterance that he was distinctly heard on North Main street.\* At the conclusion of the reading thirteen volleys were fired by the Cadets and Light Infantry; the Artillery company next fired thirteen cannon, and a like number of new cannon (cast at Hope Furnace) was discharged at the great bridge. The ships Alfred and Columbus likewise fired thirteen guns each, in honor of the day. At two o'clock the Governor, attended and escorted as above, proceeded to Hacker's Hall, where an elegant entertainment was provided on the occasion. After dinner the following toasts were drunk, viz. :

1. The Thirteen Free and Independent States of America.
2. The Most Honorable General Congress.
3. The Army and Navy of the United States.
4. The State of Rhode Island and Providence Plantations.

---

\* Mr. Brown was an Englishman, distinguished for benevolence, wit and integrity. He died in East Greenwich in March, 1785, and was interred in Providence.

5. The Commerce of the United States.
6. Liberty, to those who have Spirit to assert it.
7. The Friends of the United States in every Part of the Earth.
8. General Washington.
9. The Officers of the American Army and Navy.
10. May the Crowns of Tyrants be Crowns of Thorns.
11. The Memory of the Brave Officers and Men who have fallen in Defence of American Liberty.
12. May the Constitution of each separate State have for its Object the Preservation of the Civil and Religious Rights of Mankind.
13. May the Union of the States be established in Justice and Mutual Confidence, and be as Permanent as the Pillars of Nature.

The Artillery and a number of other gentlemen dined the same day at Lindsey's Tavern, when the following toasts were drunk:

1. The Free and Independent States of America.
2. The General Congress of the American States.
3. The Honorable John Hancock, Esq.
4. His Excellency General Washington.
5. His Excellency General Lee.
6. The Brave Carolinians.
7. Success to General Gates and the Northern Army.
8. May the subtility of the American standard destroy the ferocity of the British Lion.
9. The State of Rhode Island and Providence Plantations.
10. The Honorable Governor Cooke.
11. May the Independent States of America forever be an Asylum for Liberty.
12. The American Army and Navy.
13. The Providence Independent Companies.

"The above," says a recorder of the event, "was conducted with great order and decency, and the Declaration received with every mark of applause. Towards evening the King of Great Britain's Coat of Arms was taken from a late Public Office, as was also the sign from the Crown Coffee-House, and burnt."

Thus closed the first celebration in Providence of our nation's birth.

Of the celebration held July 4th, 1778, the Providence *Gazette* of July 11th, gives the following description:—

"Saturday last being the Anniversary of American Independence, whereby these United States through their Delegates in Congress, unanimously and forever renounced the sanguinary Tyrant of Britain, and wisely assumed to themselves a Name that is acknowledged among the Nations, the Day was celebrated here in a Manner suitable to the great and happy Occasion. At one o'clock Thirteen Cannon were discharged from the Fort on Fox Point; at Four the Forts at Pawtuxet, Field's, Kettle and Fox Points, and the ship Defence, were manned, when an irregular Fire of Cannon and Musquetry commenced, which continued near an Hour, and afforded a just and lively Representation of a General Action. The Honorable Major-General SULLIVAN with his Suite, accompanied by a number of Ladies and Gentlemen of the Town, went on board the Defence where they had a prospect of the whole Exhibition. At Sunset the Regiments stationed for Defence of the Town were drawn up in the rear of the Redoubts, and fired a *Feu-de-joi*, which did great Honor to the Director and the troops, as it was allowed by Judges to be the best Performance of the Kind they had ever heard. The vast Concourse of People that covered the Hills, and the loud and repeated Acclamations of Joy, greatly contributed to the Grandeur of the Scenes. In the Evening a number of Military Gentlemen and principal Inhabitants, assembled at General Sullivan's Head Quarters, and concluded the Celebration of the Anniversary with the following Toasts:

1. The ever memorable Fourth of July, 1776.
2. The United States of America
3. The Continental Congress.
4. Our Magnanimous Friend and Ally the King of France.
5. All the Friendly European Powers.
6. The American Plenipotentiaries at Foreign Courts.
7. General Washington and the American Army.
8. The American Navy.
9. The Governor and State of Rhode Island.
10. Protection to the State of Rhode Island, and Health to the Military Commanders.
11. A total overthrow to the Enemies of America.
12. May the Sons of Liberty enjoy Freedom in every part of the Globe.
13. May the Blossoms of Freedom never be blasted in America."

July 4, 1779. The day was commemorated "with demonstrations of joy suited to the happy occasion." Salutes were fired at the several Posts, an elegant entertainment was provided at Cold Spring, attended by Major-General Gates, Brigadier-General Glover, with several other gentlemen of the army and of the town, together with a number of ladies, and at which thirteen patriotic toasts were drunk, not forgetting Louis XVI., Generals Lincoln and Moultrie, the officers and soldiers who had died in defence of America, the United States, Congress, and the Governor and State of Rhode Island.

### A COMMEMORATION SONG.

While the patriots of Providence were engaged as above described at Cold Spring, a company of Americans, no less patriotic, were similarly engaged in Amsterdam, Holland. For that occasion the following song was written by a Dutch lady residing at the Hague. It is here reproduced, not for its poetic merit, but as an expression of the spirit which fired many sympathetic hearts in that city of Bankers, at a period when a dark cloud hung over the prospects of Freedom in our land. The tune to which it was sung is not mentioned:

1. God save the thirteen States!
   Long rule the United States!
   God save the States!
   Make us victorious,
   Happy and glorious,
   No tyrants over us:
   God save the States!

2. Oft did America
   Forsee with sad dismay,
   Her slav'ry near:
   Oft did her grievance state,
   But Britain falsely great,
   Urging her desp'rate fate,
   Turn'd a deaf ear.

3. Now the proud British foe
   We've made, by vict'ries, know
   Our sacred right:
   Witness at Bunker Hill,
   Where god-like Warren fell,
   Happy his blood to spill
   In gallant fight.

4. To our faith'd WASHINGTON,
   Brave STARK, at Bennington,
   Glory is due:
   Peace to MONTGOM'RY'S shade,
   Who, as he fought and bled,
   Drew honors round his head,
   Num'rous as true.

5. Look at Sar'toga's plain,
   Our captains on the main,
   MOULTRIE'S defence:
   Our catalogue is long,
   Our heros yet unsung,
   Who noble deeds have done,
   For independence.

6. The melting mother's moans,
   The aged father's groans,
   Have steel'd our arms:
   Ye British Whigs beware!
   Your chains near formed are,
   In spite of Richmond's care
   To sound alarms.

7. Come join your hands in ours;
   No royal blocks, nor tow'rs;
   God save us all!
   Thus in our country's cause,
   And to support our laws,
   Our swords shall never pause
   At freedom's call.

8. We'll fear no tyrant's nod,
   Nor stern oppression's rod,
   Till time's no more:
   Thus liberty when driv'n
   From Europe's States, is giv'n
   A safe retreat and hav'n,
   On our *free shore*.

9. O, Lord! thy gifts in store,
   We pray on CONGRESS power,
   To guide our States.
   May union bless our land,
   While we, with heart and hand,
   Our mutual rights defend.
   God save our States!

10. God save the Thirteen States!
    Long watch the prosp'rous fates
    Over our States!
    Make us victorious,
    Happy and glorious;
    No tyrants over us;
    God save our States!

In 1780 the day was quietly noted in Providence. A salute was fired at ten o'clock on the State House Parade by the Continental Post of Artillery, and also by an armed vessel in the harbor. At Newport, "His Most Christian Majesty's Frigate Hermoine, commanded by the Chevalier de la Touche was ornamented with a variety of colors, and fired three salutes, viz., at morning, at noon, and in the evening "

For the next five years salutes and Parades of the United Train of Artillery appear to have been the sum of public observances. In 1787 the Rhode Island Society of the Cincinnati celebrated the day, and dined at Rice's Tavern  In 1788 the town assumed the patriotic duty, and invited Rev. Enos Hitchcock, D.D., pastor of the First Congregational Church, to deliver an Oration. A military and civic street procession was a part of the display. Dr. Hitchcock's Oration (the first on such an occasion in Providence, and by request printed,) was replete with patriotic sentiment. He began by saying:

"To felicitate Americans on the anniversary of their Independence is a dictate of philanthropy. To echo among my fellow-citizens in grateful acclamations, the accession of a freed federal government, is but the natural effusion of a heart elate with joy. To sacrifice at the shrine of liberty 'the fat of fed beasts,' and pour out the generous libation, if conducted with prudence, may not be unsuitable expressions of the pleasure we this day experience.

"But a nobler employment awaits us. We ascend from gratulations and amusements to contemplate, in the temple of liberty, the various beauties of the edifice, to recount the multifarious blessings she proffers our favored land "

After a wide survey of the rise and progress of freedom, "the happy effects of the American Revolution" upon lands "far beyond the bounds of America," and the advantage it has already brought to the new nation, he closes as follows:

"We have little now to fear from our enemies, but every thing to hope from the situation, extent and resources of our country, and from the enterprising spirit of its inhabitants. Under the smiles of approving heaven may they proceed and prosper in every useful art—increasing in knowledge and virtue, until they become as conspicuous for the purity of their morals as for the equality and perfection of their government!

"May no one, this day, prove himself unworthy the freedom he enjoys, by a conduct inconsistent with the purest pleasures,—by anything unbecoming him as a man, as a Christian! May temperance, sobriety and decorum preside over all our joys, and be our constant attendants through the various walks of life. Then may we look forward with hope and joy, through all the variations of imperfect government, and the struggles of the contending passions of man, to a state of more perfect society,— to that grand community where 'universal love smiles on all around.'"

## A SEMI-CENTENNIAL.

Advancing fifty years from the day of our Nation's birth, we reach 1826, and find the fire of freedom burning with undiminished glow. It was a semi-centennial year, and "Independence Day,"— made specially memorable throughout the land by the deaths nearly simultaneously of two of the distinguished patriots and founders of our Republic, John Adams and Thomas Jefferson,—was observed in Providence with martial and civic pomp worthy the descendants of a people "born to be free." The Committee of Arrangements were Rhodes G. Allen Josiah Whittaker and Nehemiah S. Draper, who discharged their duties with excellent judgment. The day was ushered in with the ringing of bells, and the firing of national salutes from Christian Hill, Jefferson Plain, and Fox Point. The great events of the day were the public procession, and the services held in the First Congregational Church At about eleven o'clock the procession was formed on Market square, under the direction of Captain Stephen K. Rathbone, Chief Marshal, and Messrs. George C. Hale, Allen O. Peck, William H. Rodman, Samuel W. Wheeler, and Edward R. Young, Assistants.

The procession numbered more than one thousand persons, and extended from Market square to the Theatre, the present site of Grace Church. As it moved through several of the principal streets the scene was brilliant and exhilarating. First came the military escort, consisting of six companies, viz : The United Train of Artillery, Colonel Hodges ; the Independent Volunteers, Lieut.-Colonel Babcock; the First Light Infantry, Captain John J. Stimson; the Second Light Infantry, Captain Townsend; the Independent Cadets, Lieut.-Colonel Greene ; and the Fayette Rifle Corps of Pawtucket, Captain Jacobs. Following the escort were the Committee of Arrangements, Governor Cooke and suite, preceded by the High Sheriff; Orator of the day and officiating clergyman; past orators of the anniversary; clergymen of the town; Town Council, and other town officers; members of the Rhode Island Society of the Cincinnati; United States and State officers, naval, military and civil; foreign officials; officers and corporation of Brown University; Mechanics Association; Marine Society; Domestic Industry Society, and various other associations; School Committee and pupils of the public and private schools (upwards of three hundred) with their teachers; strangers, and citizens.

In the midst of this procession appeared one hundred and six veterans of the Revolution, among them a drummer beating the drum once used by him on the field of battle. This remnant of men to whom strokes for freedom at Bunker Hill, Harlem Heights, Trenton, Monmouth, Princeton, Rhode Island and Yorktown, had been familiar, was led by Captain Aaron Mann, who for gallant conduct in the retreat from Rhode Island, received promotion from General Sullivan. But to the concourse of citizens thronging the streets a special attraction was an elegant barouche in which rode the four survivors of the Gaspee exploit in 1772, viz.: Colonel Ephraim Bowen, Colonel John Mawney, Captain Benjamin Page, and Captain Turpin Smith. The barouche was drawn by four white horses, driven by Mr. Horatio Blake, landlord of the Franklin House, who volunteered the service. Over the heads of these venerable patriots waved a splendid silk banner, designed and painted for the occasion by Mr. Samuel J. Bower, of Providence, whose pencil exhibited the skill of an accomplished artist. Within wreaths and appropriate devices, bearing the names of the survivors, the " GASPEE," and the date 1772, appears a representation of the ill-fated vessel in flames, with a boat containing a number of the daring assailants rowing from the burning wreck. On the reverse are the Arms of Rhode Island, with the legend " July 4, 1776. In God we Hope. For Liberty and Independence. July 4, 1826." In the right hand corner of the obverse picture is the record by the artist: "Presented to the Committee of Arrangements by Samuel J. Bower, Pinxt."* After the celebration the Committee presented it to the Rhode

---

*Samuel J. Bower, son of John and Honor Bower, was born in Providence. Prior to and after the great September gale in 1815, he kept a dry goods store on Cheapside, North Main street. On the memorable day, when the flood had swept away the bridge connecting the east and west sides of the river, he was enabled to reach his home on Pine street only by passing up round the north side of the Cove and swimming across a narrower portion of the angry stream. Mr. Bower's father was distinguished as a carver in wood, being considered one of the most expert in his profession in the country. The "Turk's Head," which for many years looked down with becoming gravity upon passers by from its elevation on Whitman's Block, at the junction of Westminster and Weybosset streets, and which was subsequently removed and carried to the South or West, and the statue of Washington, mentioned on page 57, were specimens of his handiwork.

Island Historical Society. Fifty-four years have passed since it was used for a commemorative purpose. May it long be preserved in its present position to remind the beholder of the price paid for the blessings now enjoyed by fifty millions of freemen.*

At the church, which was thronged, the devotional exercises were conducted by the pastor, Rev. Henry Edes, D.D., who also read the Declaration of Independence. The orator was the Hon. William Hunter, of Newport; poets, Joseph L. Tillinghast, Esq., and the late President of the Historical Society, Hon. Albert Gorton Greene. Both of them wrote Odes for the occasion, which were effectively rendered by the Psallonian Society, Oliver Shaw presiding at the organ. The ode by Mr. Tillinghast was sung to an original tune composed by Mr. Shaw. The ode by Judge Greene, given below, was sung to the tune, "*Song of Mirium*"

ODE.

BY ALBERT G. GREENE, ESQ.

Joy! joy! for free millions now welcome the morn,
And hallow the day when a nation was born.
Let one song from her hills and her valleys arise,
One loud peal of triumph ascend to the skies.

---

Samuel evidently inherited from his father an æsthetic taste, and retiring from the business in which he was engaged on Cheapside, set up sign painting, a business in which he became particularly expert. His ornamental designs were always appropriate and attractive. Besides the banner above mentioned Mr. Bower painted many others for military companies. Among them was one for the Providence First Light Infantry, presented to that popular corps by the students of Brown University in acknowledgment of escort duty performed for them by the company on Commencement day. He painted another — then considered the handsomest ever unfurled — for a military company in New Orleans. The cost was upwards of four hundred dollars.

Mr. Bower entered the army in the War of 1812, and is understood to have held a subordinate command. He was on his way to New Orleans at the time of the battle there. He subsequently marched to Georgia, where he obtained some experience in skirmishing with the Indians. After leaving the army he went South and spent some time in Milledgeville and Savannah. Returning to Providence, he engaged anew in his business, which he pursued at different times on Market square, Weybosset street, and in the Hamilton and Dyer's buildings on Westminster street. The latter he occupied until his death, which occurred March 7th, 1860, at the age of sixty-three years. Mr. Bower was highly respected in the community for his moral and social worth.

*Another feature of the procession, which attracted attention, was a long timber carriage, upon which rode a large number of blacks who had served in the war of the Revolution, and had won for themselves an honorable distinction.

Let each heart and each voice join the grateful employ,
And the temples of GOD be made vocal with joy,
While the young and the aged, the brave and the fair,
Are thronging to mingle in praise and in prayer,
For those blessings which once on the field and the wave,
Were purchased with blood from the hearts of the brave,
Oh, how should the soul of the freeman expand,
To the time-honored REMNANT OF LIBERTY'S BAND:
And ye who stood foremost for freedom and right
Through your country's dark hour in the van of the fight,
Flow rich the reward which your sons have decreed
To your dauntless devotion of spirit and deed.
Your path that remains shall with garlands be strewed,
And by hands yet unborn shall the wreaths be renewed!
We have sworn that the cause which on ocean and field,
Your bosoms were bared from destruction to shield,
Through storm and through sunshine, through weal and through
  woe,
To guard unpolluted, from faction and foe,
Or, crushed in its ruins, to bravely expire,
Ere the son shall dishonor the deeds of the sire.
And think not that when all your bravest and best
In our country's green bosom forever shall rest,
That the land which ye bled to redeem and to save,
Can forget the proud name and example ye gave;
Oh no! for a million of swords shall be red,
Ere the foot of a foe o'er your ashes shall tread.
Your name will give light to the children of earth,
When they rise for a deed of true virtue and worth:
A beacon of glory, which never can die,
To cheer and to save when the spoiler is nigh.
And the land of your birth ever sacred shall be
To the HOMES to the ALTARS, and GRAVES of the FREE.

The oration, which was printed, was in Mr. Hunter's best vein. "It was worthy," writes the chronicler of the day, "of the man and the occasion, of his long established reputation as a scholar, statesman and advocate at the bar of the first order, and of the high wrought feelings and heroic associations of a day, the proudest, perhaps, in the annals of the world. For an hour and forty minutes the orator made his audience forget every thing but himself and the spirit-stirring themes upon which he dwelt with the same enthusiasm that he inspired in all who heard him."

At the conclusion of the exercises in the Church, the procession re-formed, marched to the Great Bridge, where it was dismissed, the veterans of the Revolution repairing under escort to Wilder's Hotel, where a generous entertainment had been provided for them. The subscribers to the public dinner and invited guests partook of their repast at the Assembly Rooms. Upwards of three hundred persons sat down to five tables. Colonel Daniel Lyman, President of the Rhode Island Society of the Cincinnati, presided, assisted by Colonels John S. Dexter, Benjamin Hoppin and Richmond Bullock, Gen. E. Carrington, Honorables John Pitman, Caleb Earle and Samuel Eddy, William Wilkinson and John Howland. Among those present were His Excellency Governor James Fenner and staff, the Major-General of the State Military and staff, Hon. Asher Robbins, Hon. Elisha R. Potter, Major John Vinton, field and staff officers of the Second Rhode Island Brigade, and other military gentlemen. Twenty-four regular, and a number of volunteer, toasts were drank, and patriotic post-prandial speeches were made by Joseph L. Tillinghast, Esq., and Hon. Asher Robbins. The chronicler already cited, says: "The day passed off in the most acceptable manner, and though our streets have never witnessed a more brilliant parade, or a greater collection of people, there was scarce an instance of intoxication or wrangling that occurred. Early in the evening the streets were deserted."

### HISTORICAL TRACTS.

The Soldiers and Sailors Historical Society, of Providence, have deposited with this Society, a series of tracts, ten in number, published by it, elucidating interesting and important events in the War of the Rebellion. By the authority of the Society the Treasurer has subscribed for the series of Rhode Island Tracts now being published by Mr. Sidney S. Rider. This insures to us publications that will soon be out of print, and the value of which, from their scarcity, will in the future be greatly increased.

### OUR WANTS.

While we recognize in our collections many important works of history, biography and genealogy, we are made painfully conscious of deficiencies in these several departments. There are many works of a local and general character that we ought to possess, which past experience has shown we are not likely to receive as donations. A small sum annually appropriated for the purchase of such works would gradually supply a want constantly felt.

That the Rhode Island Alcove is deficient in the classes of publications above referred to, is no just cause for unfavorable criticism. It is to be borne in mind that from the organization of the Society until some years after the erection of the Cabinet in which we are now assembled, there were but few persons in the State sufficiently interested in the objects of an Historical Society to voluntarily aid its work. This general indifference rendered it peculiarly difficult to obtain accessions to its collections. The Society had no means with which purchases could be made of valuable books and pamphlets even then becoming rare, while many such were owned by persons unwilling to part with them for any pecuniary or other consideration. The work of the successive librarians, Judge Staples, and Judge Greene, was gratuitous, as similar labors have continued to be. The pecuniary resources of the Society did not warrant opening the Cabinet except at quarterly meetings, and at such other times as papers could be procured to be read. Yet with all the drawbacks and discouragements early experienced, the Society, through its officers, did a noble and praiseworthy work. Judge Staples, Judge Greene, Dr. Webb, John Howland, Thomas C. Hartshorn, and others, were indefatigable in their efforts to secure every description of Rhode Island literature, no less than every class of manuscripts that might be helpful in elucidating Rhode Island history and genealogy. The "Foster Papers," the Moses Brown and other papers, numbering more than twenty thousand, were secured. At a subsequent period a large portion of them were collated, mounted and bound, and thus put in condition to be safely examined and used. The invaluable files of the Providence *Gazette*, from its commencement, a duplicate set ·of which no money could now purchase, were made its property, while a number of valuable aboriginal and other relics of early times found a place among its treasures. It built for itself this structure, a work of many years' struggle, and the first Historical Society in the country to own a home. Its six volumes of collections, its ten or more addresses, its eight annual Proceedings, that have been printed, and its frequent aid to authors, show that it has not been at any time supine. Other facts equally honorable might be stated, but it is unnecessary. The Society in the past needs no apology. All familiar with its paucity of means at the beginning, the slow growth of public sympathy for it, and the difficulties it has had to encounter at almost every step of its progress, will honor it for what it has accomplished, and at this hour rejoice that the hope of still better days may be entertained.

As already intimated we have wants, and not the least of them is an addition to this building. Such a building should be suited to the uses of a lecture room and picture gallery, as also for the exhibition of treasures which at present cannot be well displayed. Had we a room of this kind, there is little doubt but valuable paintings would be donated to the Society, or placed on permanent deposit. The subject has long occupied the thoughts of many of the actively interested members of our Society. If the present may not be considered the most propitious time to move in this matter, it is to be hoped that again calling attention to the want may be helpful in ultimately securing its supply.

### CONCLUSION.

Although much has been done to lay open the early history of Rhode Island, much remains to be done to give completeness to its details. Not only are there in our own State many sources of information not yet explored, but beyond its borders is to be found material with which to illustrate the personal, social and civil life of our little commonwealth. It is said that the Registry of Deeds in the County of Suffolk, Mass., contains records of deeds of land in Rhode Island, copies of which ought to be in our archives. There are doubtless other papers to be found in Massachusetts, having a bearing upon the history of this State, to which this remark applies. The same is true of records and private papers in Connecticut and New York. To gather up these fragments that nothing be lost, is eminently the work of this Society. Should there be any delay in inaugurating it?

During the year now closed I have communicated with nearly three hundred persons, in this State, soliciting contributions for our Society. The results have been gratifying and encouraging. I desire here gratefully to thank those who have cordially and promptly responded to my requests. My hope is that the year before us will prove no less prosperous than the year from which we part.

Respectfully submitted,

EDWIN M. STONE,

*Librarian and Cabinet Keeper, Northern Department.*

JANUARY 13, 1880.

# REPORT

#### OF THE

## PROCURATOR FOR NEWPORT.

---

NEWPORT, R. I., January 10, 1880.

*To the Rhode Island Historical Society:*

During the past year but little, comparatively, has been done in Newport in the way of historical research. The Newport Historical Society has had but few meetings, but additions have been made to its collections; and through the zeal and energy of its Librarian, Mr. James E. Manran, many documents, which might otherwise have been lost or destroyed, have been secured and placed in the archives. The books and papers belonging to the Society he has arranged and classified, and he has labored to make good the files of old colonial newspapers, and imperfect sets of other printed matter.

An effort has been made to secure a series of biographical sketches of distinguished Rhode Islanders, and it has so far borne fruit that one volume, the "Life and Works of Gilbert Stuart," has been published. This field might be worked more profitably. Surely there is material enough to write extended lives of men like Theodore Foster, William Vernon, and others whose names are readily recalled in this connection, but whose biographies have yet to be written.

In the library of Yale College there is a Diary, kept by Rev. Ezra Stiles, and which extends over the years that he resided in Rhode Island. It is full of historical facts connected with the Colony, and it is greatly to be regretted that it has never been printed; or, at least, that some person, properly qualified, has not been employed to copy, with the sanction and approval of the Trustees of the College, all such passages as are of direct interest to the historian. It is five and twenty years since I saw it, but I remember that with the text there are diagrams, drawn with pen and ink, explanatory of some of the skirmishes between the English and the Americans. I feel sure that if the historical matter in these pages were sifted out the means expended in this way would be well employed.

I would most respectfully ask that some decided steps be taken by the Rhode Island Historical Society to push forward the branch of historical research to which I have called attention; that we may secure, at least, sketches of men whose names have come down to us, where there is not material enough for full biographies. The older citizens of the State, men who could furnish information on this and other branches of our history, are fast passing away, and if we would gather from them the facts with which they are familiar we have no time to lose.

GEORGE C. MASON,
*Procurator for Newport.*

# REPORT

### OF THE

## PROCURATOR FOR BRISTOL.

BRISTOL, R. I., January 13, 1880.

*Amos Perry, Secretary R. I. Historical Society, Providence:*

DEAR SIR.—As Procurator for Bristol County, I do not find any matter of particular interest to communicate to the Historical Society at its annual meeting to be held this evening.

At the annual town meeting in this town in April last measures were inaugurated for a proper observance of the bi-centennial settlement of the town, which occurs in September of the present year. A general committee was appointed, who promptly met and organized, and have succeeded in raising a sum of money to aid in defraying the expenses of the proposed celebration. Other steps are being taken to add to this fund, which it is hoped will, together with such sum as the town may appropriate, be sufficient for the purpose. Professor J. Lewis Diman, of Providence, has been invited to make the historical address, and Rt. Rev. M. D'W. Howe, of Western Pennsylvania, to prepare a poem for the occasion. It is understood that both gentlemen have favorably responded to this call from their native town. As the time approaches it is hoped that the interest will correspondingly increase.

In Warren there has been some talk of erecting a monument to Massasoit, who pledged his faith to the Pilgrims within a few months after their landing at Plymouth, and faithfully kept it for more than forty years until his death in 1662. When Edward Winslow visited Massasoit, in the summer of 1621, he found the latter's home and wigwam on the banks of the Sowams river, near a living spring of water, which is now known as Massasoit's Spring, at the foot of Baker street in the town of Warren. There has been some discussion and difference of views expressed as to the most appropriate location for the monument, but it is to be hoped that this will not long delay the consummation of this highly meritorious project.

Very respectfully yours,

WILLIAM J. MILLER.

# REPORT

## OF THE

## COMMITTEE ON GROUNDS AND BUILDING.

The Committee on Grounds and Building respectfully submit their report of expenditures made during the year 1879:

| | |
|---|---:|
| Paid Robinson Pierce, for labor and lumber in making additional room in the basement for the storage of books, papers, etc., | $31 21 |
| Paid W. S. Hogg, for care of the grounds, for rolling, cutting grass, etc., including $21 60 for work done in 1878, - - | 49 57 |
| Paid for oiling front door, $1 25; painting lamp over the gate, $2; washing floor, $1.50, - - - - - | 4 75 |
| | $85 53 |

For the Committee,

ISAAC H. SOUTHWICK,
*Chairman.*

PROVIDENCE, January 13, 1880.

# REPORT

## OF THE

# COMMITTEE ON GENEALOGICAL RESEARCHES.

*To the Honorable Rhode Island Historical Society, January, 1880:*

The Standing Committee on Genealogical Researches beg leave to report:

That, although no very prominent measure has been set on foot by the Society itself, we have reason for great encouragement in the zeal with which various members are prosecuting enquiries in this department, and the very general and rapidly increasing interest in this direction, which pervades the public mind, and also from the constantly accumulating publications which add materially to our facilities in this interesting and important pursuit.

The Committee beg leave especially to congratulate the members of the Society on so momentous a consummation as the publication of the Registration of the Town and City of Providence, and to express their profound sense of the merits of that work, and the obligation conferred on the Society and the public by the compiler and publisher thereof, and to suggest to the Society that a vote of thanks would be a just and well merited tribute to the diligence and public spirit of those gentlemen.

The Committee again beg leave to reiterate the views heretofore expressed that the whole people of the State are equally interested in the preservation and publication of all the original town and church registrations and collateral records bearing upon the subject, and cannot cease to urge that every method should be used to impress upon the public mind that legislative action, to this end, is legitimate and proper, and by that alone can it be thoroughly and successfully prosecuted.

All which is respectfully submitted by

HENRY E. TURNER,
ZACHARIAH ALLEN,
WILLIAM A. MOWRY,

*Committee.*

# REPORT

## OF THE

## COMMITTEE ON PUBLICATIONS.

The Committee on Publications of the Rhode Island Historical Society beg leave to suggest to the Society the publication of a seventh volume of its collections. It is now thirteen years since the publication of volume six. The Society was never in a more flourishing condition than at the present time; its meetings are frequent and well attended, and an increasing interest is manifested in the preservation of books and manuscripts relating to our early history.

Among the collections of the Society, hidden from sight, your Committee think that papers of value exist which should be printed. They beg leave, therefore, on the occasion of the fifty-eighth annual meeting of the Society, to call attention to the subject, in order that if deemed practicable, early steps may be taken for the publication of another volume, the seventh of the Society's collections.

JOHN R. BARTLETT,
J. LEWIS DIMAN,
EDWIN M. STONE,
*Committee on Publications.*

PROVIDENCE, January 13, 1880.

# REPORT

#### OF THE

## COMMITTEE ON THE STATE APPROPRIATION.

The Committee on State Appropriation, appointed at the meeting of this Society in April last, respectfully report:

The sum of $282.54 dollars has been received from the General Treasurer of the State, in accordance with the appropriation.

The rooms of the Society have been kept open daily, between the hours of ten and one, and of two and five, except during the short days;—the expense of this being $29.16$\frac{2}{3}$ per month, or at the rate of $350 a year.

The books and papers belonging to the State, in keeping of the Society, have been marked and catalogued, as required by the statute.

Some attempts have been made to obtain the records of certain towns, for the purpose of copying the same,—without success at present, but with better prospects for the future.

Pamphlet-cases have been bought by the Committee for the use of the Society.

The newspapers belonging to the State, and those belonging to the Society, have been examined and catalogued, and list of numbers wanting has been made.

Respectfully submitted.

CHARLES W. PARSONS,
JOHN H. STINESS,
GEORGE T. PAINE,
*Committee.*

PROVIDENCE, January 13, 1880.

# NECROLOGY

## OF THE

## RHODE ISLAND HISTORICAL SOCIETY.

## 1879-80.

---

WILLIAM GREENE WILLIAMS, son of Mathewson and Mary (Greene) Williams, was born in Johnston, R., I., November 21, 1798, and died at his residence on Washington street, Providence, March 16th, 1879, in the eighty-first year of his age. He early lost his mother, but received the best of care from a step-mother, of whom he always spoke in terms of warm affection.

In 1812 he entered as a clerk in the dry goods business in Providence, and in 1819 engaged in business for himself. After successful enterprise for thirty-three years he retired from active trade, and devoted the residue of his life to historical and genealogical investigations. He was particularly interested in whatever related to the settlement of Rhode Island, and to the lives and experiences of its early settlers. He traced his descent on the paternal side thus: Mathewson, Andrew, Jeremiah, Joseph, Joseph, Roger Williams. On the maternal side his register was: Mary Greene, (his mother,) daughter of Joshua, Samuel, Samuel, John, John. His grandmother was Mehitable Manton, daughter of John, Edward, Shadrach, Edward. He traced his pedigree back to Gorton Coggeshall, and at least a half dozen other original settlers. Each of his numerous ancestors he could place in their respective order, from memory, and probably few men living were so familiar as himself with the genealogy and history of the numerous original families in the State. In his favorite pursuits he visited grave yards and various historical sites, and procured records, regardless of time and expense. The knowledge he thus acquired was cheerfully imparted to others.

In business relations Mr. Williams was a man of the strictest integrity, and nothing disturbed him more than to witness in men, or in the management of financial institutions, any departure from uprightness. He held his word to be as sacred as his bond, and was freely outspoken when he discovered in others a departure from this high standard of rectitude. It was a pardonable pride with him to be able daily to say, "No man is suffering in consequence of any pecuniary dereliction of mine." He held in marked contempt shams of every description, and appreciated with corresponding strength of feeling a true sincerity in professions of friendship. He had long made human character and the hidden springs of action a careful study, and could quickly detect the real from the seeming. In congenial circles he found much enjoyment, and often recalled with expressions of satisfaction the agreeable people he had met in his summer excursions. For many years he was a great sufferer from a disease that was slowly but surely sapping the fountain of life. But his will power was great, and he endured where many would have sunk. Of the change that was gradually approaching he was fully aware, and for some years before his departure he had been disciplining his mind for the event.

He became a member of this Society in 1858, took a deep interest in its affairs, and for many years served its interests faithfully as a member of the Committee on Building and Grounds, and as a member of the Committee on Nominations.


NICHOLAS REDWOOD EASTON, son of Nicholas and Dorcas C. Easton, was born in Providence, and died at his residence, Central Falls, Lincoln, March 24th, 1879, in the sixty-ninth year of his age. He was of the firm of Easton & Burnham, spindle manufacturers. He had been confined to the house for several months, but had not been in good health for a number of years. He was a member of the Congregational Church in this village. For nearly a score of years he has lived and done business in this community, and won the respect of all who knew him, as a straight forward, upright business man; one whose word was as good as his bond. He was of a quiet yet genial disposition, and we do not believe he had an enemy. He will be missed by his family, by relatives and friends, by the church of which he was a consistent member, and by the community where his life of integrity has been marked and approved.

The funeral was solemnized from his late residence on Broad street, March 27th, at eleven o'clock, A M Rev. J. H. Lyon, of the Congregational Church, officiated. The remains were taken to the North End Cemetery, Providence.—*Central Falls Visitor, March 28, 1879.*

Mr. Easton was elected a member of this Society in 1878.

WALTER PAINE, son of Walter and Lydia (Snow) Paine, was born in Providence, and died at his residence in this city May 14th, 1879, in the seventy-eighth year of his age. Mr. Paine for many years was clerk of the Supreme Court in Providence County, subsequently entering the insurance business, and for the past twenty-eight years he has been officially connected with the Merchants Insurance Company. He has repeatedly represented the city in the General Assembly; was two years Justice of the Police Court; was member of the Common Council seven years, and one year President of that body; and was Alderman for the fourth ward in 1858–59. All his public and private trusts were administered with fidelity and intelligence, and he leaves the record of a good citizen and an honest man.

About two months preceding his death Mr. Paine was taken with a severe attack of some form of paralysis, from which he partially recovered, and for a week or ten days was again regular in attendance at his place of business. Two days before his death he was at the office the last time, when he remained for three hours. The next morning, at 6 o'clock, he was taken with a second attack, and from that time remained in a torpid state until the time of his death. Mr. Paine was one of the persons named in the charter of the Merchants Insurance Company, and at the meeting for organization, May 15th, 1851, was chosen Secretary, which position he filled for sixteen years. In June, 1867, upon the resignation of President Comstock, Mr. Paine was chosen President, and remained so up to the time of his death. His term of service with this company was twenty-eight years, lacking one day, and all the time the office was in the What Cheer Building, where it was opened before the building was finished.

Mr. Paine was married September 23d, 1823, to Miss Sophia F. Taylor, who bore him seven children, five of whom, with his widow, survive. He was elected a member of this Society in 1875.

COLONEL ROBERT GROSVENOR, son of Dr. William Grosvenor, was born in Providence, November 2d, 1847. After completing his preliminary studies he entered Norwich University, at Northfield, Vermont, where he was graduated in June, 1868. In 1876 the degree of A. M. was conferred upon him by his Alma Mater, and at the time of his death he was one of the Trustees of the University. Colonel Grosvenor was trained to business in the office of the Grosvenor Dale Company, and discharged most usefully and acceptably the duties of his position, giving promise of a successful and honorable career as a business man. In 1869 he became a member of the Marine Corps of Artillery, of which, in 1871, he was made Adjutant, in 1872, Second Lieutenant, in 1873, Junior Major, and in 1874, Lieutenant-Colonel commanding. For this corps, as also for the Marine Corps Veteran Association, Colonel Grosvenor cherished a warm interest, and did much to promote their welfare. In July, 1879, he was stricken with typhoid fever, which terminated fatally on the nineteenth of that month, causing a deep and painful void in the domestic relations, and filling a wide circle of friends with sorrow. Colonel Grosvenor, at his decease, was in the thirty-second year of his age. In social life he was genial, courteous, and in the highest sense of the term a manly man. He left a wife but no children. Immediately on the announcement of his death the Marine Corps and Veteran Association met at their armory and passed resolutions appreciative of his character, and tendering sympathy to his bereaved family. As a husband, son, brother, citizen, friend and business associate, he filled the measure of each requirement. The funeral, which took place Monday noon, July 21st, was numerously attended, the Marine Corps of Artillery and the Veteran Corps being represented. The services at the house, and at the family ground at Swan Point Cemetery were conducted by Rt. Rev. Bishop Thomas M. Clark, D.D., LL.D., and Rev. David H. Greer. The casket in which the body reposed was covered with flags, and the floral offerings were numerous, and were arranged with great taste and beauty.

Colonel Grosvenor was elected a member of this Society in 1872.

GEORGE THURSTON SPICER, a well-known and respected stove merchant and Alderman of the city of Providence, was born in Hopkinton, R. I., August 4th, 1802. His father was a farmer who improved a large tract of land, and was also proprietor of the Village Hotel, which, with its host, is thus pleasantly described in a diary published nearly fifty years ago:

"In the village of 'Hopkintou City,' so called, where I stopped several months, was an inn, kept by a church member, and now aged landlord, Captain Joseph Spicer, a man of the most unbending honesty, whose full fare for man and beast, and his ready and urbane attention to the wants of the weary traveller, gave him as far as he was known the reputation of 'a good host.' But what struck my attention with no little interest was the sign in front of the house, suspended from the limb of a noble sycamore. At the top was a beautiful eagle, the emblem of our independence, over which was a cluster of stars. Directly underneath was seen the anchor, emblem of hope. At the base of the picture, in rich gold letters, were the words, 'In God we Hope,' the only sure guarantee of individual or national safety. With such a hope was America once made free, and with it shall always remain so."

Alderman George T. Spicer was the son of Captain Joseph and Mary (Saunders) Spicer, and one of a family of six children. He was early trained at home in habits of industry and self reliance, receiving also such public instruction as the village school afforded. He was scarcely twenty years old when he received a commission from Governor Gibbs as Captain of the first company of Hopkinton Volunteers, which he held for several years, when, desiring to learn the trade of a machinist, he resigned his commission and commenced work at the village of Potter Hill, about four miles distant. While here he became a member of the Seventh Day Baptist Church, for which he always cherished warm interest and affection. After learning his trade he removed to Phenix, in the town of Warwick, where he remained seven years, having charge of the machine shop a part of the time, and discharging his duties with the most exemplary industry and fidelity. He was also the first Superintendent of the Sabbath School at Phenix, started about this time (1827). In an article on the Hon. Charles Jackson, published in the Providence *Journal*, January 24th, 1876, the writer thus pleasantly alludes to the work which Mr. Spicer was then doing:

"That cheerful, bright, and I was going to say OLD gentleman, (but he is only seventy-three, and never seems to me to be older than forty when

I meet him,) our Alderman Spicer, was then a young machinist at work for Daniel Gorham at 'the Phenix.' He was employed by Governor Jackson and his brother to make the machinery and looms for their mills. He had never seen a power loom, and tells a good story of how he got sight of one. It was at the Anthony Mill. While he was busy examining it, the overseer came and ordered him out, but he had seen enough to enable him to construct one."

Mr. Spicer was afterwards employed in Providence for a short time at the machine shop of Thomas J. Hill, when, in 1830, he removed to Pontiac, in the town of Warwick, where he became connected, as superintendent, with the mills and bleachery of John H. Clark, retaining full charge till he moved to Providence fifteen years later. He also had charge at Pontiac, of the school affairs of the district.

In October, 1833, Mr. Spicer married Mary Sheldon Arnold, daughter of Horatio and Celia Arnold, and grand-daughter of Judge Dutee Arnold, of Warwick, who served the State as Associate Justice of the Supreme Court from 1817 to 1822. In April, 1845, Mr. Spicer permanently removed, with his family to Providence, where he became interested in the manufacture of stoves and furnaces. He was Superintendent of the High Street Furnace Company for five years. In 1850, he, with his brother-in-law, Dutee Arnold, and Zelotes W. Holden, erected a new stove foundry on Cove street, and laid the foundations of the successful business with which he retained an undiminished interest up to the time of his death, which occurred at his summer residence at "Fort Hill," Pawtuxet, August 17th, 1879. We copy the following editorial article, concerning his business and official life, from the Providence *Journal* of August 18th, 1879:

"George T. Spicer, the head of the house of Spicers & Peckham, a venerable and much-respected citizen, died yesterday morning, after a brief illness. Although still engaged in the active labors and duties of life, Mr. Spicer had reached his seventy-eighth year. He has continuously represented the fourth ward in the Board of Aldermen since 1870, (having previously served in the Common Council,) and was twice elected President of the Board. Mr. Spicer also represented the city several years in the lower house of the General Assembly. He brought to the discharge of his public functions broad general information, good ability, the habits of a well trained business man, and loyalty to what he believed to be right. In business and social and domestic life he was greatly respected and beloved. Born in Hopkinton at the beginning of the century, he was familiar with Rhode Island history, tradition and sentiments, and his conversation upon past men and 'times abounded in pleasant personal reminiscences and unwritten political information."

From the same paper, 21st inst., we quote:

"The funeral services were conducted by his pastor, the Rev. J. G. Vose, D.D., of the Beneficent Congregational Church, who impressively dwelt upon the integrity, purity and industry of the departed life, his faithfulness and tender affection for his family, and his reverence for religion, and constant attendance upon worship."

We will only add, that during a long life, in eventful times, he maintained a character for independence and honesty, without being a partizan, and secured that good name which is to be chosen above riches.

Mr. Spicer was elected a member of this Society in 1878.

JOHN OLDFIELD, son of William and Mary Oldfield, was born in Bradford, England, March 9th, 1796. He was one of a large family of children, and early manifested a taste for horticulture. Several years of his minority were devoted to perfecting himself in the knowledge and practice of scientific gardening. On arriving at his majority, he emigrated to this country and located in Philadelphia, where he remained a number of years pursuing his profession. From that city he removed to New York, and there followed the same occupation for a short time. Thence he went to Charleston, S. C., where he spent six months, and in 1824 came to Providence, where he at once entered the employ of the late Thomas P. Ives as gardener. At the end of four years he engaged in the lumber business on his own account, which he prosperously pursued for about twenty-five years, when he retired from it, and purchased a farm in Cranston. This he managed for some time, but the last twenty years of his life were devoted to the care of his property and his family, and enjoying the society of his friends. His extensive travels made him a pleasant and instructive companion. He married Martha Sampson, daughter of Earl Sampson, a prominent citizen of Assonet, Mass. His wife, two sons and two daughters survive him. Mr. Oldfield had warm sympathies for the poor, and his unostentatious charities will be greatly missed by many who partook of his bounty. He became a member of this Society in 1865, and was a very constant attendant upon its meetings. He died January 8th, 1880, in the eighty-fourth year of his age.

BENJAMIN GLADDING PABODIE, son of William and Henrietta (Gladding) Pabodie, was born in Providence December 1st, 1799, and died at his home in the same city January 25th, 1880. His ancestor, John Paybody, with three sons and one daughter, emigrated to this country from England about 1635. With his youngest son William, (of whom the deceased was a direct descendant,) he is named among the original proprietors of Plymouth, Mass., and in 1645 their names appear among the owners of Bridgewater. William removed to Duxbury where he owned much land and filled many public offices; he was one of the purchasers of Sakonet or Little Compton, and removed thither in 1684.

William's wife, Elizabeth, was the third child and eldest daughter of John Alden and Priscilla Mullins, whose story is told in Longfellow's "Courtship of Miles Standish."

In the fourth generation, Ephraim, the grandfather of the deceased, moved from Little Compton, where the family had flourished for over sixty years, to Providence. The remainder of the family, following the law of immigration, gradually went westward, until naught but the gravestones remain to perpetuate the name in the old town.

The subject of this sketch attended school at the Academy at Bank Village in Smithfield, kept by David Aldrich. He there met with an accident which, after years of confining and painful sickness, resulted, in his seventeenth year, in the amputation of one of his legs. Upon his recovery, he assisted in the business of his father, who for many years carried on the manufacture of fur hats, and also had two stores for the sale of those and kindred goods,—one on High street, the other on Market Square. About 1825 he went into the retail hat and fur business for himself on Maiden Lane in New York city, but not meeting with success he soon returned to Providence, and opened a similar store there. He removed to the Arcade, on its completion in 1828, where he remained until 1861, removing then to No. 39 Westminster Street, and finally retiring from active business in 1863.

He was a member of the Common Council of Providence from the first ward during the years 1851 to 1854, inclusive.

He was elected to the General Assembly of the State in the spring of 1866, and served during that and the following year.

He was Trustee of the Reform School in 1854; and served as Director of the Arcade Bank from July, 1833, and after its acceptance of the provisions of the National Bank Bill and change of its name to Rhode Island National Bank, until 1876.

He became a member of the Rhode Island Historical Society in 1870, and a life member in 1874.

He married February 4th, 1836, Frances Hayward Blackman, who died October 1st, 1854, leaving one son who still lives; and November 15th, 1858, he married Lucy Ballou Taft, who survives him.

Hon. SAMUEL GREENE ARNOLD, son of Samuel Greene and Frances Rogers Arnold, was born on the 12th of April, 1821, in Providence, in the house on the corner of South Main and Planet streets, made famous in local history as the rendezvous of the band of patriots who there made their final arrangements for the capture of the British schooner Gaspee, commanded by Lieutenant William Duddington, and which was accomplished June 9th, 1772. In this assault Lieutenant Duddington was wounded, being the first blood shed preliminary to the American Revolution.

In his early boyhood Mr. Arnold attended a school kept by Messrs. Crane and Keely. He was afterwards a pupil of Prof. George W. Greene, and was subsequently under the instruction of private tutors. From them he passed to Dr. Muhlenberg's school at Flushing, Long Island. He entered Brown University and graduated in the class of 1841. In 1848 he was elected a Trustee of the University, which office he held at the time of his decease. He was called to fill various offices of responsibility, and as a member of the School Committee, as a Trustee of the Butler Hospital, as a Trustee of the Reform School, as a member of the Franklin Society, as for sixteen years an active member of the Fire Department, and as President of the Charitable Baptist Society, he rendered faithful and efficient services.

After leaving the University Mr. Arnold entered the law school at Cambridge, and at the close of his legal studies received the degree of LL.B. While in college, and during a vacation, he travelled in the West, where his health became impaired by an attack of yellow fever. For this cause he was obliged to leave college and cross the ocean to recruit. He went, accompanied by his pastor, the Rev. Dr. Hague, as far east as Greece and Constantinople. His next visit to Europe was after graduating from college, and, while pursuing mercantile studies, he went as supercargo in a vessel to St. Petersburg. In 1845 he went again to Europe, and extended his journey through Egypt and the Holy Land. It was during this absence that he went to Norway, and was only the second

American who had visited the North Cape. In 1846 he was for the second time at Constantinople. In 1847 he crossed from Europe to South America, where he passed a year in making himself acquainted with the history, social life and material resources of that country. Here he formed a pleasant acquaintance with many distinguished personages, among them Gen. Bartolomé Mitre, a historian, poet and publicist, and Don Domingo Faustino Sarmiento, afterwards Argentine Minister to the United States, and subsequently President of the Republic. In 1865, while on a visit to Providence, Don Sarmiento was the guest of Mr. Arnold, and delivered a discourse before the Historical Society on North and South America.

In 1869 Mr. Arnold went again to England, where he spent several months. His various journeys furnished him with materials for several interesting and instructive lectures, which were read in this city and elsewhere. Among these was one on "The Pampas of South America;" one on "Peru;" and one describing his "Journey to the North Cape." The results of his observations were embodied in an interesting Essay, and in 1851, published in the *North American Review*.

Although Mr. Arnold received the honors of the Cambridge Law School, his legal studies were not pursued with a purpose of practising at the Bar, but rather to gain knowledge that would be helpful as a mental discipline, and promote habits of accuracy in thought. His fondness for literary pursuits, especially history, was early developed, and he was led thereby to a pursuit that has placed him prominently before the public as a historian. In 1853 he delivered a discourse before this Society on "The Spirit of Rhode Island History," which foreshadowed the acumen that characterizes the two elaborate volumes that followed it in 1859 and 1860, viz : the "History of the State of Rhode Island and Providence Plantations," dedicated to the people of the State as a memorial "of the trials and the triumphs of their ancestors." In preparing this work, exhaustive examination of public archives, both at home and in London and Paris, was made, as well as of all available printed works and private papers, leaving little or nothing of vital importance to be gleaned by future historians. Seldom has so much of detail been crowded into a State history, while its general accuracy will give it an imperishable place among works of a similar character. The other published writings of Mr. Arnold were "Memorial Address on Judge Albert G. Greene, Judge William R. Staples and Dr. Usher Parsons;" "Centennial Anniversary of Building the First Baptist Meeting-house;" "Centennial History of Portsmouth;" "Centennial Fourth of July Oration before the Municipal authorities and citizens of Providence;" and "Centennial Address Commemorative of the Battle of Rhode Island."

Thrice Mr. Arnold was elected Lieutenant-Governor of this State,— in 1852, 1861 and 1862. In the last named year he was chosen by the General Assembly Senator to Congress, to fill out the unexpired term of Hon. James F. Simmons, the duties of which office he discharged with uncompromising fidelity to the Union.

When, in 1861, the assault upon Fort Sumpter, indicated but too plainly the disturbed condition of the country, Lieut.-Gov. Arnold offered his services to Governor Sprague, who placed him upon his staff with the rank of Colonel. As such he took the general command of "The Marine Artillery" until after it reached Washington. In passing Alexandria, then in the hands of secessionists, danger was apprehended; but by a well devised strategy the steamer upon which the battery was embarked reached the capital without molestation.

On his return from South America, in 1848, Mr. Arnold was united in marriage to Miss Louisa Gindrat Arnold, daughter of his uncle Richard J. Arnold. Mrs Arnold and three daughters survive to mourn his loss.

In 1844 Mr. Arnold became a member of the Rhode Island Historical Society. In 1845, under the original organization, he was elected a Trustee, a position held by him until 1849. From 1855 to 1868 he held the office of a Vice President. In 1868 he succeeded the late Judge Albert G. Greene as President,—his two predecessors, like himself, dying in office. His classical training, his extensive travels, his familiarity with men and events, his pronounced opinions on public affairs, his keen sense of right, his quick recognition of social proprieties, his high ideal of honor, his consistency in friendships, his urbanity, and his readiness to impart information by whomsoever sought, eminently qualified him for instructive companionship, and for the acceptable discharge of public duties.

For several years prior to the decease of Mr. Arnold a gradual weakening of the vital forces was perceptible. Journeys to a more genial climate, if they retarded, did not stop the progress of disease, and in the winter of 1879 the rapid approach of its final issue was made painfully manifest to solicitous friends. But in the prospect before him he was calm and self-possessed. "In his last illness," writes one whose accurate delineation of Mr. Arnold's life and character appeared in the Providence *Journal* on the morning after his decease, " it was observed how quick and warm was his appreciation of the kind attentions of his friends. The pain and sore weariness of wasting disease he bore not only without complaining, but with patience and cheerful courage. When his friends were sad and depressed by his bedside, it was the patient himself who came to their relief with some bright, uplifting remark, uttered in the same familiar tones they had been wont to hear in the days of his health and strength. In the full possession of his faculties to the last, he made all his arrangements with calmness, as if for some journey he was about to make. Accustomed to contemplate thoughtfully the issues of life and the realities of the hereafter, he looked to the coming inevitable hour with composure and with expectation, in submission to the will of Heaven. And so has gone from among us another of our worthiest citizens. Not only by those who were nearest to him, and in the midst of whom he died, but by many others, too, will he be missed and mourned. But he leaves behind him the memory of an upright, honorable and generous character, and of many valuable services, which he loyally rendered to his native city and State."

Mr. Arnold died at the Narragansett Hotel in Providence, where, with his family, he was temporarily residing, February 13th, 1880. On the afternoon of the following day, the Historical Society met to take becoming notice of the sad event. A minute to be entered on the Society's Records was presented by Professor William Gammell, which he supplemented with a discriminating notice of the deceased. Remarks were also made by Professor J. Lewis Diman, and the writer of this brief sketch, drawing attention to the striking characteristics of Mr. Arnold. The minute was then unanimously adopted.

The funeral services of the deceased took place February 16th at the First Baptist Meeting house, in the presence of a very large audience, among whom were Governor Van Zandt, Secretary of State Addeman, members of the State legislature, His Honor Mayor Doyle, members of the city government, and members of the Rhode Island Historical Society. The services, simple, appropriate and impressive, were conducted by Rev. Drs. Ezekiel G. Robinson, Samuel L. Caldwell, and William Hague, each of whom made touching addresses. The remains were interred in Swan Point Cemetery.

E. M. S.

# THE CONDITIONS OF LIFE,

## HABITS AND CUSTOMS,

OF THE

# NATIVE INDIANS OF AMERICA,

AND THEIR

## TREATMENT BY THE FIRST SETTLERS.

---

## AN ADDRESS

DELIVERED BEFORE THE

## RHODE ISLAND HISTORICAL SOCIETY,

DECEMBER 4, 1879,

BY

ZACHARIAH ALLEN.

# HISTORICAL ADDRESS.

### THE INDIAN AGE OF STONE.

The recent discovery of an ancient Indian manufactory of stone pots and smoking pipes near Providence, and the persevering researches of Rev. Frederic Denison and of Mr. Charles Gorton, have excited fresh interest in the early history of the Indian race. The admirable collection of more than a thousand specimens of artistic stone-arrow-heads, hatchets, chisels, pestles and mortars, and also of shell beads of different colors, exhibited before you, are memorials of the race of red men who once owned and occupied the beautiful isles and shores of Narragansett Bay, and are now passed away. These implements of stone are evidences of their progress in the useful arts, and of their degree of civilization. While they have disappeared, their thoughts and deeds remain engraved on these imperishable stones. So the petrified remains of plants and animals, found on our planet, are the "sermons in stones," that, as pre-historic records, show the exercise of divine intelligence and power.

The first exercise of human skill and intelligence was early manifested by modelling the abundant quartz and flints on the earth's surface into various tools and implements subservient for useful purposes in the arts of war and peace. For this reason the primeval stage of human existence has been characterized

### THE AGE OF STONE.

Stone implements, such as arrow heads, hatchets, pestles and mortars, etc., now displayed before you, have been found on different parts of the earth, resembling those made by the New England Indians.

The quarry of soft soapstone, or steatite, near Providence, offered facilities for modelling this material into various useful vessels, as pots and pipes. The extent to which this quarry has been worked by the Indians is manifest by the excavations which the present proprietor* states once formed apartments under cover of the shelving cliff. There workmen might have been employed as in a manufactory. But no metallic implements of bronze, of Indian manufacture, have here been discovered, such as were found among the native Indians of Mexico, when discovered by the Spaniards in 1492. The Indians there had so far progressed as to be able to extract metals from ores of copper and tin, and to melt them together to produce bronze. This compound is rendered nearly as hard as steel for cutting wood and granite, by being cast into cold metallic moulds *to chill* it, as practised at the present day, in chilling cast iron and bronze. The native Mexicans had thus made a progress in the useful arts, which has been classed as

### THE AGE OF BRONZE.

Their second stage of human progress included also skill in the manufacture of gold and silver vessels, of textile fabrics of cotton, wool and flax, dyeing cochineal red, and also of interweaving the bright feathers of parrots and of humming-birds into gorgeous mantles, that were prized by the ancient dames of Spain, as they now are by modern ladies. The age of bronze in Mexico, and in Egypt at an earlier date, appear to have been nearly similar, as neither had progressed to the third stage of

### THE AGE OF IRON.

The natives of India and China appear to have made the earliest progress in the use of iron and steel, as well as in the manufacture and dyeing of cotton fabrics, wool and silk. The silks of India were early prized in Europe at nearly the value of their weight in gold. Fine India muslins were of such a gossamer texture as to leave the contour of beautiful forms half revealed beneath folds of transparent drapery. The porcelain of china also surpassed that of Europe during the past century, and still remains admirable as "china ware." The Chinese were the first to utilize steel for magnetic needles for guiding vessels across pathless seas, and travellers across the great steppes of Asia.

Then the Greeks progressed in the use of steel in the art of war, and were thus enabled to dominate over the less skillful nations of the earth. The serried ranks of the Macedonian phalanx, armed with glittering steel, and led by Alexander, marched triumphantly to the regions of India.

* Horatio N. Angell.

Afterward the superior skill of the Romans in the use of steel swords predominated over the civilized world, with a facility graphically described by Cæsar in the memorable words, "*Veni, vidi, vici*,— I came, I saw, I conquered!"

Since then, this paramount power in the use of steel implements of war has been acknowledged by international law as supreme "by the right of conquest."

After a time the relaxation of Roman vigor by luxury enabled the hardier nations of the North to predominate, and then came the decline and fall of the Roman empire. Next followed the great improvement effected by combining the use of iron implements as guns, for rendering efficient the explosive force of gunpowder. In this invention the Turks took the lead in the fourteenth century by capturing Constantinople from the Romans,—by besieging Vienna, and threatening to overrun Europe. They fitted out Barbary corsairs, which spread terror along the shores of the Mediterranean, and the adjacent Atlantic. All christians (as infidels) were captured and sold as slaves, unless ransomed. One of the original settlers of Providence, William Harris, was captured by a Barbary corsair on his voyage to Europe, enslaved, and finally ransomed by the Connecticut colonists, in whose service he was employed. Thus Carthage once ruled the waves, as Britannia has since, by superior efficiency in the use of iron and gunpowder on the high seas.

In the recently published biography of Admiral Farragut it is stated: "In 1558 the Turks carried off four thousand of the inhabitants of the coast of Italy, including his ancestor, Antonio Farragut, his wife, and six children; who were ransomed and returned to Italy after six years' captivity." What a contrast does this event afford to the superior power wielded by their descendant on the waters at New Orleans and Mobile.

The maritime countries of Europe long continued to pay tribute to the Barbary States, until the skill and courage of the people of the United States of North America finally compelled the Crescent to yield to the Cross, by boldly attacking the fortified ports of Tripoli and Algiers; whereby Europe was relieved from further tribute.

The early superiority of the Turks in the effective use of cannon and fire-arms was realized by me on visiting the arsenal of Constantinople, in the year 1851. Among the specimens of ancient arms, there were breech-loading cannon and guns, and revolving fire-arms, which antedate these inventions by any other people. These rude specimens of fire-arms exhibited a remarkable contrast, when compared with the improved breech-loading rifles, of which six hundred thousand were recently furnished to the Turks from the workshops of Providence, to repel the Russian invaders. The rapidity of discharging rifle balls from these improved guns, with a range nearly equal to that of artillery, and a precision that is marvellous, has essentially changed the old systems of warfare, and of artillery practice, and is destined hereafter to determine " the course of empire."

Had a few of these rifles been available on the classic fields of Troy, near Constantinople, where Homer's heroes, gods and goddesses, contended in a ten years' war, Jupiter might have preferred a repeating rifle to a zig-zag thunderbolt, and Ulysses have "got through and gone home," before he was forgotten by his wife.

The dexterity of the Spaniards with their superior steel weapons in exterminating the natives of Central America is described by Las Casas, Bishop of Chiapa, who was an eye witness of their actions: "The Spaniards, mounted on horses, and armed with steel swords and lances, committed the most horrible slaughters with impunity. They passed through the towns, killing women and children as well as men. They laid wagers one with another, who could cleave a man down most dexterously with his sword, or take off his head from his shoulders at one blow, or run a man through most effectually. They hanged thirteen of these poor heathen in honor of Jesus Christ and his twelve apostles. They erected scaffolds upon forked poles, and laid the chiefs and principal men upon them, and kindled a slow fire beneath to cause the most exquisite anguish and outcries." "By the barbarous cruelties inflicted by the Spaniards on the aborigines in Mexico, they exterminated more than eleven millions of them within forty years after the discovery of America."

The Spaniards, under Philip II, inflicted similar exterminating cruelties on the Protestants in the Low Countries, and Protestants, Jews, Gentiles, and Mohammedans, all alike, have used their predominant physical power in exterminating, by martyr fires and cruel deaths, others of different religious creeds, denoted " heathen."

To resist this general instinctive propensity of the more powerful to dominate over the weaker, swords were formerly worn by the sides of civilized men, and *revolvers* at the present day. The human species having no natural weapons for self defence, as horns, claws, tusks, or stings, are necessitated to seek out many inventions for strengthening "their hands to war, and fingers to fight." For mutual protection of the weak against the strong, various species of animals associate together in flocks and herds, and the human species unite as fellow citizens in communities; whereby the power of the whole population is employed to protect each individual. This is civilization. The advantages of Roman citizenship, or civilization, was manifest in the appeal of St. Paul against the cruelties of the Jewish priests.

After the christian nations of Europe improved their steel implements of war, reinforced by gunpowder, they in turn began to dominate over other nations of the earth, as the Romans and Mohammedans had previously done  When the Spanish rulers sent out Columbus to take possession of America, " by virtue of his christianity," the Pope in Rome actually made to them a free gift of the whole continent from pole to pole, with all the people and their property; which was certainly a very munificent gift. Then all other christian nations joined in the general scramble, by sending out maritime expeditions for plundering heathen countries.  Royal licenses were granted to buccaneering adventurers, " to take possession of any lands or property not previously subjected to any christian prince or people." The great wealth of the infidel people of India early attracted the notice of the steel-armed Greeks under Alexander, and then of the Mohammedans.  The proverbial wealth of "the great Moguls" was a tempting prize to the European christians, and especially to the Italian merchants and navigators of the fourteenth century, who were engaged in oriental commerce.  It became the day-dream of the Italian navigators to reach India or Cathay directly, by sailing westward.  To accomplish this purpose an Italian navigator, Columbus, prevailed on the Spanish rulers in 1492 to fit out vessels to make the passage direct.  He stumbled on the intervening continent of America, which barred his way; but was very successful in plundering the heathen natives of Mexico of their gold and silver, and other property, accumulated in their ancient cities.  This success stimulated a second Italian navigator, John Cabot, to go to England, to promote another attempt to reach Cathay by a direct passage by sailing westerly in a more northerly latitude.  Cabot induced a company of English merchants to fit out an expedition in 1496, four years after that of Columbus.  They obtained a license or royal patent from Henry VII, in consideration of one-fifth of the profits accruing to him. He gave them authority under the British flag " to sail over the seas and seize any lands or countries not previously possessed by any christian people."

John Cabot made the attempt to reach Cathay by sailing to the icy coasts of Newfoundland, and then by proceeding southerly along the coast.  He failed in finding a passage; which was fortunate for the people of India, who were thus saved from the spoliations inflicted by the Spaniards on the American Indians.

Central America, when first discovered, was supposed to be a part of India, and hence that region was called "West India," and the natives were denoted "Indians."

A third Italian navigator, John Verazzano, came to France twenty-eight years later (1524) and urged the royal rulers to renew the attempt to find a direct passage to India. He sailed directly to the present capes of Virginia, and from thence explored the coast as far as Maine and Newfoundland. He published an account of his entering the mouth of the present Hudson river; which was seventy-five years afterward settled by the Dutch under the English navigator, Hudson. Verazzano from thence followed the southern coast of Long Island, passed Block Island, and entered Narragansett Bay. There he anchored, and remained fifteen days in exploring its shores and islands. He was the first European who ever beheld the land where we now dwell,—unless credit be given to the legends of the Northmen. He describes the natives as being "the goodliest people we have found, being liberal and friendly, but unacquainted with the use of iron." "They are clothed in dressed leather skins and furs. The women modestly refused to leave the canoes to come on board our vessel. The shores and islands of the bay are covered by forest trees."

Continuing his voyage along the coast around Cape Cod, he describes the natives there as being "suspicious, hostile, and desirous of obtaining steel implements for defence against kidnappers; who frequented the coast to seize and transport them for sale as slaves to the Spanish planters in the West Indies. There being no gold or silver here to reward the navigators, as in Mexico, and only a few furs and skins for traffic, the buccaneers, for profit, had recourse to the capture of the natives for slaves: as has been the case in ages past on the coast of Europe by the Mohammedans, and on the coast of Africa by all other nations. Imbued with the belief of the right of ownership, founded on superior might of arms and conquest, all the first maratime adventurers from Europe considered the lives and property of heathen people to be subjected to their peculiar use.

The first settlers of New England began to kill and sell the natives at their pleasure.

After despoiling the Mexicans and Peruvians of their gold, silver, and other wealth, accumulated in their Age of Bronze, the Spanish adventurers and cavaliers sighed for other similar regions to conquer,— an Eldorado somewhere in the interior of North America. Ponce de Leon and De Soto made raids from Florida and traversed wild forests only to find poor, uncivilized natives, armed with bows and stone-pointed arrows, and possessed of no valuable property. These adventurers obtained food by plundering the Indians, and found graves beneath the forest shades. De Soto was buried in the turbid waters of the great river Mississippi, which he was the first of Europeans to discover. The poverty of the natives saved them from the continued presence and oppressions of the invaders.

The whole coast of North America, from Florida to Maine, offered no inducements to tempt Europeans to settle therein, except for agriculture. Labor and toil were not relished by the first maritime adventurers, who brought with them only swords and fire-arms, and no hoes or ploughs for tilling the soil. After the lapse of nearly a hundred years of repeated exploring expeditions in vain attempts to reach the coveted wealthy regions of India, the French people appear to have been the first to commence a more rational system of trading with the natives for skins and furs, and especially for embarking in the profitable cod-fishery on the New England coast. To carry on these honest business pursuits, they sent vessels under Jacques Cartier, in 1534,— eighty-six years before the first settlement of Plymouth in New England,— to make permanent locations on the sea-coasts adjacent to the cod-fisheries, and to establish trading posts among the interior tribes of Indians on the great river St. Lawrence and on the great lakes, over to the river Mississippi.

Jacques Cartier narrates that he was " entertained near Montreal by an assemblage of Indians, with a feast of corn, beans, squashes, pumpkins, and fishes." This statement shows that the aborigines of North America were an agricultural, not merely a nomadic people, living by the chase and fishing.

The importance of the cod-fishery on the coasts of Newfoundland and " New England " as first named by John Smith in 1606, was manifested by " the employment of more than four hundred fishing vessels from Europe in this profitable business so early as the year 1583."

The island of New Foundland being convenient for a permanent fishing station, a company was organized in England by Humphrey Gilbert under the first English royal patent, granted by Queen Elizabeth, "to take possession of any remote lands not occupied by any christian prince or people, and to exclude all persons from coming to settle within two hundred leagues of any place he might occupy," the queen " reserving a right to share one-fifth of all the profits."

Gilbert made a permanent settlement in Newfoundland, and, by right of discovery by John Cabot, secured the possession of that island, with all its coal mines, to England. He was accompanied by his step-brother, Walter Raleigh; who obtained another patent from Queen Elizabeth, two years later (1585), for establishing a colony further south under a milder climate on the American coast, and with a similar exclusive right "to all territory within two hundred leagues of his settlement." Two vessels were fitted out by the company of merchant adventurers in London, which carried out emigrants destined to settle north of the Spanish settlement in Florida. They were landed on the coast near Roanoke, which they named "Virginia," in compliment to their virgin queen.

Mr. Bancroft describes these adventurers to have been "broken down gentlemen and libertines, more fitted to corrupt a republic than to found one. There were very few mechanics, farmers, or laborers among them." They carried out swords and fire-arms, like the previous Spanish and French adventurers to Florida, to win their living, instead of earning it by labor. They immediately began to seize the provisions belonging to the natives, and proved themselves to have been a *buccaneering* association of communists by plundering and enslaving the natives, and uniting in a Joint Stock London Company, to divide the profits of their plunder.

Although armed only with arrows and spears, the natives resisted their invaders successfully, and not one of them was left to tell the tale of their extermination when the next company of adventurers arrived.

The second company, pursuing the same course of plundering, was nearly exterminated. More than three hundred and fifty were massacred in one night. Having brought no agricultural tools for producing their own food, and the feeble natives having fled to the forests, the few surviving colonists were reduced to such a condition of starvation, that "the living had not strength to bury the dead decently, and the bodies were trailed out for burial like dogs."

Based on communistic and socialistic principles, the Virginia Company failed of success, until this system was radically changed to that of individual self interest, by a division of the land, under the direction of Captain John Smith, of Pocahontas celebrity. He induced the directors to apportion lots of land in plantations for each one of the colonists; whereby, as historically stated, "every man, working for himself, produced more than thirty working for the common stock." He instituted systematic industry for self support, instead of the wild and adventurous career of which their chivalrous and talented leader, Sir Walter Raleigh, had been an eminent example, with the termination of his life on a scaffold, in 1602, after devoting it to colonizing enterprises and expending £40,000 in vain.

Immediately after abondoning the system of plundering the native Indians, and reorganizing the colony on the basis of individual self interest, labor, and economy, the Virginia settlers began to thrive by raising corn and tobacco, making turpentine and resin, and exporting timber. Thus rendered independent and comfortable, they became desirous of making there a permanent home, and being lonesome, like Adam in paradise without a 'wife, but not being, like him, furnished with a supply ready at hand, they found it necessary to send out orders for them to London. The cost of importation is described as having been established at one hundred and twenty to one hundred and fifty pounds of the staple article of tobacco; which appears to have been about the average weight of the articles imported. "Some of the first families in Virginia," history states, "are descended from these first settlers."

After the rational system of labor and self dependence had been established by John Smith, Gates, and others, the colonists began to throw off their dependence on the English rulers, and to elect their own officers, and the first representative assembly was chosen in 1619. But the buccaneering principle of enslaving the natives of America was transferred to enslaving the natives of Africa in 1618; which subsequently cost the lives of a million of freemen fully to abolish.

After the commencement of a system of self government in the Virginia Colony, the further services of the old directors in London became so obnoxious to the people, that in 1623, the royal Virginia patent was formally cancelled, and the company dissolved.

In the depressed condition of the Virginia Joint Stock Company, after the decapitation of their leader, Walter Raleigh, Captain John Smith returned to England, and commenced a project of retrieving the financial condition of the company by securing a monopoly of the profitable codfishery on the coast of New England. He proposed to plant a colony on the adjacent shore of " Cape Cod," and then to claim the monopoly of this lucrative fishery under the broad patent of the Virginia Company, by excluding all others from coming within " two hundred leagues of their colony." Accordingly John Smith was sent out by the London Directors to explore the New England coast, in order to find the most favorable location for a fishing station. Aided by Ferdinando Gorges he went from the present border of Maine to Cape Cod in an open boat, and made a chart of the coast. He selected the port of Plymouth, and gave it its present name.

This project being favored by Captain Gosnold and Gorges, the Virginia Company advertised shares in this new joint stock company, under their old patent, for ten pounds per share to capitalists, and for seven years' personal services to actual settlers, with a division of the land and profits at the end of seven years. Their advertisements reached some English refugees, who had fled from England to enjoy the exercise of their peculiar religious principles, in Holland, that glorious country of religious freedom. Their leaders, Mr. Bradford and Mr. Robinson, state that they were kindly received, but the emigrants became restless because their younger members intermarried with the Dutch, and their English language was yielding to the Dutch language. The refugees, who assumed the name of Pilgrims from their second removal, appointed John Carver to contract with the London Directors of the Virginia Company; and many of the very poorest bound themselves to seven years of personal service in the colony as a commutation for the ten pounds per share, and also to find their own food and clothing. In accordance with this contract, no supply of food or tents were provided, and the emigrants were landed in mid-winter on the cold New England coast, and left to care for themselves. The natural result was the death by exposure and starvation of nearly half of these Plymouth colonists during the first winter.— precisely as had occurred in the two previous attempts of this "Virginia Company" to colonize. Thus were these poor emigrants deluded by the advertisement of the London Joint Stock Company, and instead of sharing in profits and the division of lands, equal in extent to the whole of Holland, they found graves on a sandy bluff of the sea-shore.

The grasping London Directors not only attempted to obtain the possession of a great region of territory on the land, but also a monopoly of the adjacent fishery on the high sea, within the designated "two hundred leagues of their settlement." They thus calculated both to plunder the Indians of their lands, and also their fellow-countrymen of their common law rights on the open sea. To carry out this purpose they prevailed on the authorities to send out an English Admiral to enforce their claim, and drive off any vessel approaching the coast without their license. It was this blockade that prevented any vessels coming to the port of Plymouth, and consequently prevented the first settlers from obtaining supplies from the numerous fishing vessels on the adjacent sea, although, as Morton states, there were more than seventy at one time near them.

Having brought no supply of provisions with them, the Pilgrims immediately after landing used their swords and guns to carry out the original purpose of taking possession of the country and property of the natives. The historian of Plymouth, Morton, narrates: "The first explorers found fair baskets of corn and beans in the Indian houses, which they brought away without paying for. The Indians defended their property with bows and arrows until the bullets splintered the bark of trees, behind which they were sheltered; when they sprang away with a yell."

One of this exploring party, Mourt, narrates: "We found houses furnished with bowles, dishes, and trays, made of *wood*. There were earthen pots, baskets ingeniously ornamented with shells of black and white colors, wrought together in pretty work. Among useful household stuff were ornamented things, such as deers' horns, shells, and eagles' claws. There were provisions of corn, beans, dried fish, and tobacco. Outside were bundles of flags, bulrushes, sedges, and other materials for manufactures." "The houses are built of poles, arched over at top, with an opening for the smoke. The inside was neatly lined with mats." He continues: "The best things we brought away with us, including ten bushels of corn and beans. And truly 'twas God's Providence we found these things in our starving condition."

The natives, armed with their bows and arrows, fled from the superior efficiency of the guns and swords; which were then rendered useless for forcibly procuring bread, and could only be used for killing game. Had not a supply of shell-fish been obtainable on the shores, Mr. Palfrey states they must have nearly all perished in the winter.

The assaults and robbery of the natives excited their hostility, and rendered them "enemies," as the first settlers made them, and called them from the outset. As an immediate consequence of a fear of retaliation, it is narrated: "Their sufferings by hunger and cold during the winter were augmented; for during their weakness and wants, they were necessitated to employ their feeble strength to inclose the settlement with a palisade, and to barricade their dwellings." "They even carefully smoothed over the numerous fresh-made graves of their companions, to conceal from the Indians the diminished numbers and weakness of the survivors. The few survivors had scarcely strength to attend the dying." At one time, "a man could not halloo at night without creating a general alarm of an onslaught by the enemy."

That the first settlers of Plymouth brought these troubles upon themselves is proved by the subsequent friendly course manifested by the adjacent Indians. After the famishing Plymouth settlers, in the ensuing spring, were reduced by hunger to the necessity of acting like christians, in sending payment to the Indians for the corn they had robbed them of, and of offering to pay them justly for more, then the Indians not only brought them corn, but showed them how to plant and raise it for themselves.

That the Indians of New England were naturally endowed with gentle as well as grateful feelings, is proved by the kindness and hospitality of the Sachem Massasoit, the chief of the natives near Plymouth. Roger Williams, as a christian missionary, visited him, and labored to improve and benefit his people. Years afterward, when Williams was proscribed by the Massachusetts Puritans, he fled to the hospitable shelter of his wigwam, and was kindly entertained there during fourteen weeks in midwinter. And Canonicus, the same old Narragansett Chief, who defiantly sent a bundle of arrows tied together by a rattlesnake skin, to the Plymouth settlers, gratefully requited the kind treatment of Roger Williams by freely giving to him, when banished, the land where the city of Providence is built, and where we now have our pleasant homes. Thus it appears that though the Indians had only weapons of stone, yet they had not hearts of stone.

In like manner the first settlers of Hartford obtained, in their extremity, during the first year after their arrival, a cargo of corn from Canonicus. By pursuing the course of christian justice and kindness to the Indians, the people of Rhode Island ever lived amicably among them; and until the four United New England Colonies made an exterminating war against them, Williams affirms: "I cannot learn that the Narragansetts have ever stained their hands with any English blood, either in open hostilities or secret murders. Many hundreds of the English people have found them inclined to peace and love. Through all their lands many a solitary Englishman has travelled alone with safety and loving kindness. Hath not the God of peace and Father of Mercies made these natives more friendly to us in this their own country, than our fellow-countrymen in our native land?"

Edward Winslow stated in a letter: "We have found the Indians very faithful to their covenants of peace with us, very loving, and ready to pleasure us. We go with them fifty miles into the country, and walk as safely in the woods as in the highways in England. Though not professing religion, they are trusty, quick of apprehension, humorous and just."

Cushman writes: "To us they have been like lambs; so kind, trusty and submissive, that many christians are not so sincere."

Had the first settlers of New England been wholly actuated by christian principles of "peace and good will to men," instead of being involved as adventurers in rapacious joint stock companies, by the false and delusive representations of their promoters, a very different history of their character and conduct might have been recorded.

When the real intention of the directors of the Virginia Company to enforce a monopoly of the fisheries on the New England sea-coast became known, they were strenuously opposed by the English merchants and members of Parliament, and immediate measures were adopted to defeat the attempt. A new royal patent was forthwith applied for and obtained from King James, in November, 1620, even while the Mayflower was on the way to New England. This royal patent constituted the original basis of the "Massachusetts Bay Company."

After arriving at Plymouth, so remote from the original locality of the Virginia settlement, the Pilgrim emigrants became immediately aware of the deception practiced upon them, which was shuffled off upon the captain, as having been "bribed by the Dutch to land them on the New England coast." Realizing that the Virginia patent was worthless authority for founding a colony in New England, the emigrants held a meeting in the cabin of the Mayflower before landing; and in this emergency no other course was left than to make an immediate agreement among themselves for the regulation of their conduct, and submission to such leaders as the majority might appoint. This simple agreement, written and signed on board the Mayflower, constituted their original democratic form of government under the common law of England. Before they had entered into this covenant in the cabin of the Mayflower they were legally subjected to the new charter granted by King James to another set of directors in the southwest of England. But having become organized and in actual possession of that part of the country, the Plymouth Colony was left to its own control without interruption for many years until their final union with "the Bay."

In forming the New England Colony, John Smith narrates: "I labored to bring together the western merchants and the London Virginia Company, but found that each desired to be lord of the fisheries. To induce emigrants to go to New England, and leave the comforts of the English homes, I believed that no other motives than profit would determine them."

The patent granted by King James to the New Western Company included an extraordinary extent of territory, authorizing them to hold exclusive possession of all the land lying between the fortieth and forty-eighth degree of north latitude, and extending from the Atlantic to the Pacific ocean,—then called "the South Sea." This grant covered territory already in possession of the Dutch on the Hudson river, and French in Maine and along the river St. Lawrence to the great lakes, and even to the Mississippi river. "This Massachusetts Patent included more than a million of square miles, capable of containing a greater population than Europe then contained."* "Without permission of this new company of 'the Council of Plymouth,' not a vessel was allowed to enter a harbor between Newfoundland and the latitude of Philadelphia, nor a skin to be bought of an Indian, or a fish caught on the coast; or even an emigrant to tread on their soil." Bancroft adds: "A royal grant of such a vast extent of the American continent without regard to the rights of other nations and individuals, excited the amazement of Englishmen, and the scorn of powerful nations. This grant was illegal, as a violation of the constitutional laws, by contravening the common law rights of all Englishmen. It was protested against by Sir Edward Coke in Parliament, as concealing plans of private profit under color of public good, in planting a colony."

Mr. Bancroft further adds: "The maritime adventurers of those days, joining the principles of bigots with the boldness of heroes and pirates, considered the wealth of the countries which they might discover, as their rightful plunder, and the inhabitants, if christians, as subjects;—if infidels, as their slaves." "Experience shows that corporations, whether commercial or proprietary, are the worst sovereigns; gain being their object If skillfully administered, the colonists are made subservient to commercial avarice, and are pillaged by faithless agents. Corporate ambition is deaf to mercy and insensible to shame."

Mr. Palfrey says :† "It would be an error to suppose that the community at Plymouth was strictly of a religious character. The London Joint Stock Company had business objects, and was by no means solely swayed by religious sympathies There is no proof that these Leyden people had any control in the selection of their copartners. One of them, John Billington, was afterward hung for murder; and two others were punished

* Bancroft's History of the United States, ch. v.
† History of New England, ch. v.

for fighting with swords and daggers. Of the twenty-seven who survived the first winter after being landed from the Mayflower, eleven only were favorably known. All the rest are either known unfavorably, or only by name."

But certainly their piety and self-sacrifice in leaving their native land and fleeing to Holland for the purpose of there enjoying religious freedom entitles them to esteem and veneration.

The Dutch rulers offered to transport the English emigrants to their colony in New York, and to allow them the same freedom of public worship they had enjoyed in Holland; but it appears they could obtain no other guaranty of the same privilege in America than the assurance, "there are no bishops to persecute you." They chose New England rather than the Dutch colony at New York, because, as they averred, they desired to preserve their English language and relationships. They became copartners in a grasping London company for sharing in the profits of seizing Indian lands, and their owners as heathen slaves, and for obtaining a wrongful monopoly of the fisheries on the adjacent sea. With a desire to believe paternal ancestors were solely actuated by religious motives in coming to Plymouth, the inflexible records of the early history of New England demonstrate that they came to America like the myriads of emigrants who have since arrived here, for the primary worldly purpose of bettering their condition in life.

To judge aright of their motives and action, it is necessary to revert to the circumstances and times when speculative maritime adventurers obtained buccaneering licenses for sailing over the seas to capture and plunder feebler countries.

A recent report of the civil service in Great Britain affirms: "Charters and monopolies, in a fit of good humor, were once tossed by a king to some favorite person at court, who might have pleased him; and these patents were as arbitrarily revoked in a fit of anger or drunkenness. An English king could once enrich a great baron or favorite, not only with spoils of foreign lands, but with those of fellow subjects. The great lords and ecclesiastics looked down haughtily upon the half-enslaved common people. Reactions against such tyranny culminated in the riots under Watt Tyler, Jack Cade, and in the rebellion under Cromwell; and finally in the execution of King Charles. America was given away, and colonized under royal grants and patents to trading monopolists."

Pilgrims and Puritans alike, by virtue of their christianity, assumed themselves to be the saints of the Lord, and that "the earth, with the fulness thereof, is the Lord's and the inheritance of his saints." They practically attempted to establish the Jewish doctrine in the new world which the Saviour came to abolish in the old world, in accordance with the precept: "The law was given by Moses; but grace and truth came by Jesus Christ."

After the unsuccessful experiment of carrying out these doctrines in Virginia and Plymouth, few emigrants were willing to make another similar experiment in Massachusetts. A few fishermen located themselves at Naumkeag, (Salem), under Mr. White and Mr. Conant in 1628, and Endicott was sent out there in 1629, by the new company in England; but the hardships of a fisherman's life on the ocean waves deterred new settlers from joining this small settlement, especially after learning the sufferings and miseries of all similar joint stock colonists under the management of a board of directors in England. Emigrants were unwilling to leave the comforts of their English homes and the security under English courts, to subject themselves to the arbitrary power of mercenary joint stock directors, three thousand miles away. Having realized that the Virginia and Plymouth colonists had never prospered while they continued to be ruled by directors in England, and that they immediately began to thrive after the management of their affairs was placed in the hands of the colonists, to elect their own officers, the new company of the Council of Plymouth in England despaired of success, unless they allowed similar privileges of self-government to induce emigrants of wealth and influence to embark for settling their proposed colony on Massachusetts Bay. The English directors proffered to actual settlers not only the privileges of self-government and of titled offices of distinction, but also the unimaginable extent of profits from sharing the Indian lands from the Atlantic to the Pacific oceans, which constituted the capital stock of the new Massachusetts Bay Company. The idea of becoming independent rulers in New England, as governors, legislators, judges, etc., and of obtaining titles of honor and profits, from which they were excluded by the civil and ecclesiastical aristocracy in Old England, was fascinating to wealthy and ambitious men. Coveting such distinctions and honors, laymen and clergymen alike now ardently came forward to seek their fortunes in the New World.

As it was entirely contrary to the policy and feelings of the royal rulers and Parliament of England to concede any formal grant of independence to the colonists, this result could only have been brought about indirectly, by considering the settlers to be members of an incorporated joint stock company, to which the appointment of agents and other officers is commonly conveyed by legal acts of incorporation, as being essentially necessary for the judicious management of their affairs. To accomplish the proposed plan of establishing an independent company on the shores of Massachusetts Bay, the directors of the Council at Plymouth in England sold to Sir Henry Roswell, John Young, John Humphrey, John Endicott, and about forty others, a portion of their vast original patent; "bounded northerly by a line three miles north of every part of the river Merrimac, and by another line three miles south of the river Charles and the Massachusetts Bay, and extending westerly from the Atlantic to the Pacific ocean."* This long and narrow belt of land somewhat resembled a tape line in relative dimensions. To give a color of authority to the conveyance "the signature of King Charles I. was obtained after much labor and expense." "To his eyes the transfer was only that of a trading corporation." "Not a single line alludes to freedom of religious worship."†

These liberal terms, with advertisements of the profits from sales of lands, and of the pleasures of free hunting and fishing on their own lands, excited such a rush of emigrants, that nearly three thousand came over in 1629 and 1630; including gentlemen of wealth and influence, and clergymen. John Winthrop was elected governor, and the civil government was organized. The ministers, Skelton and Higginson, who were clergymen of the Church of England, organized also an independent ecclesiastical government. These clergymen, who had taken an affectionate leave of their "dear mother church" on embarking, after disembarking cast off their dear old mother for a new step mother, by a speedy wedding between their reörganized church, and the State of Massachusetts. They at once began to exercise their usurped ecclesiastical power as supreme rulers, or popes in Boston. This was protested against by two brothers, Brown, shareholders in the Massachusetts Bay Company. They were arrested by the civil rulers on complaint of the co-ecclesiastical rulers, and were sent back to England by the same vessel that brought them, with warning that "this is no place for such as you." They only desired the liberty of going to church as they had been accustomed to do. For this reason, Mr. Bancroft affirms, "Episcopacy had no inducements to emigrate to Massachusetts, for it was only Puritanism that emigrated to obtain ecclesiastical power." The ecclesiastical power then usurped by Skelton and Higginson was maintained in Massachusetts two hundred years, until finally abolished by a popular vote, establishing the Bill of Rights, that now ex-

* Prince, 247.   † Bancroft, vol. i, p. 343.

empts all persons from being taxed to support any church which they do not attend.

To strengthen their authority by connection with the civil power of the State, the ministers in Boston, like the priests in Jerusalem and the Pope in Rome, assumed to be interpreters of God's will, and thus established a kind of Theocracy, enforcing their doctrines with the frequent use of the term, "Thus saith the Lord."

That the Puritans did not come to New England to establish "religious freedom" and "for conscience' sake," as is commonly maintained by their descendants, was immediately manifest by their commencing to persecute the Baptists, Quakers, and other dissenters.

The principal motives that induced our forefathers to come to New England, as previously narrated, were the profits of the sea-coast fisheries and the possession of a great extent of land under the royal license, denoted a Patent. The immediate motive of the emigration of the wealthy and influential leaders was personal ambition to better their condition in life, and to act as independent rulers in the new world.

That the main object of the first settlers of New England was the profitable coast fishery is evidenced by their early suspending a huge codfish from the ceiling of their General Assembly room, over their heads, as a memorial of their devotion to their staple business pursuit. This Puritan codfish is still reverently preserved by their descendants in Boston, and may be now seen suspended over the heads of the representatives in the State House, covered with the dust of ages. The ancient Jews similarly set up and idolized a golden calf as an emblem of their devotion to their staple business of raising cattle. Likewise a great bale of wool is placed conspicuously in the House of Lords in England, and the presiding officer mounted thereon, to serve as an emblem of their devotion to the principal staple manufacture of Great Britain.

"The pursuit of fishing is an honest and honorable business," as affirmed by the King on signing the royal patent, "for it was the avocation of the early christian disciples." The seizing possession of the Indian lands without compensating the owners, as was expressly enjoined on the grantees of the royal patents, was not an honest or honorable business, and was opposed by the teachings of Roger Williams. For opposing the unjust seizure of the Indian land, which affected the pecuniary value of the capital stock of the Massachusetts Bay Company under their patent, Williams was indicted for treasonably "teaching certain strange doctrines, denying the authority of the magistrates," and sentenced to be sent back to England by a vessel then ready to sail; precisely as the brothers Brown had been sent back for similarly denying the authority of the ministers in Boston.

The following protest was addressed by Williams to the rulers at a later date:

"In the sight of God you will find this question at bottom to be, *First*— a depraved appetite for the great vanities, dreams and shadows of this vanishing life by the acquisition of great portions of land in this wilderness; as if men were in great necessity and danger for want of land, like the poor thirsty and hungry seaman on a starving passage. Land is one of the gods of New England, for the idolatry of which the Most High will punish the transgressors."

Having practically realized the despotic power wielded by the union of church and State, it thenceforth became the life-long labor of Williams to found a new colony upon the constitutional basis of separation of the ecclesiastical from the civil power. At that time the established church of England predominated in Great Britain under the rigid rule of Charles I. His tyranny excited the rebellion that caused his execution in 1649, and the subsequent triumph of Puritanism in England under Cromwell. The Massachusetts colonists, in becoming independent of the British rule in church and State, in 1630, set up a new independent dynasty for themselves, in which Puritanism superseded the old established church with increased exacting rigor. During this period of revolutionary troubles in England, the little colony planted by Williams at Providence struggled for existence, in villages governed by mutual and conventional agreements on democratic principles. In 1643 an act of incorporation of Providence, with several towns under one government, was obtained. As historically stated, "the settlers were careful to conciliate the good will of all the Indians who claimed any sort of interest in the lands. Those who had built wigwams, or tilled the soil, received gratuities, in addition to what had been paid to the sachems. Confirmatory deeds from the successors of the first grantors were obtained; every new deed requiring some further gratuity." Amity was thus maintained, and the settlers built their houses alongside of the Indian wigwams.

The Rhode Island colonists continually struggled against the encroachments of the Four United Colonies around them, until a royal charter was obtained, in 1662, from Charles II, granting them civil and religious freedom. The King desired to secure religious freedom for public worship to the Catholics in England, and gladly signed the charter conveying this privilege to the people of the little colony, as "a lively experiment" for showing that a civil government may best be established and maintained with a complete freedom of opinion in all religious concernments. The Puritans in England delayed the final passing of the charter under the great seal, fearing that this liberal concession might be a precedent for the free worship of the Roman Catholics; but "the roaring of the lion finally prevailed and brought it about," as Williams narrates.

A similar resistance to the establishment of religious freedom in England was made afterward by the sectarians, when James II. attempted to proclaim religious toleration for the benefit of all dissenters from the established church, including the Roman Catholics. "A convocation of the leading dissenters thanked his majesty for his courtesy, but answered, they preferred to remain as they were. Then the King tore up with his own hands the proclamation he had prepared."* The ecclesiastics verified the origin of their name from the original Greek word, EKKLEIO: *I exclude*.

To prevent ecclesiastical tyranny in our republic the people made the first amendment to their constitution, forbidding "any establishment of religion, and any law prohibiting the free exercise thereof."

The adoption of the Monroe Doctrine, in 1823, virtually checks the arrogant assumption of absolute power by Europeans over the land and people of America, as they have been accustomed to do in ages past. The last attempted was by a French emperor to place Maximilian on a throne. By opposing the right of European maritime adventurers to seize the lands and property of the Indians in America, Roger Williams appears to have taken the lead in this Monroe Doctrine, as well as in establishing freedom from ecclesiastical tyranny in the separation of Church and State.

While the leaders of the New England settlers have often erred in not adhering to principles of justice and christian beneficence, the common people have steadfastly persevered with intelligence and skill in making the wilderness to blossom as the rose. They have manifested vigor and virtues that have honored the human race.

Relying on the gratitude of the Indian chiefs for his sacrifices in their cause, Williams fled from his home in Salem in mid-winter, to escape deportation, and sought shelter beneath the hospitable roof of Massasoit in Warren during fourteen weeks. The grateful sachem gave to the refugee a tract of land on the eastern shore of the Seekonk river by the side

---

* Neal's History of the Puritans.

of a little cove. After planting corn there, Williams was notified by Governor Winslow that this location was within the bounds of the Massachusetts patent. He was then provided with another tract of land by the Indian chief Canonicus, on the west side of the Seekonk river, beyond the boundary line of the Massachusetts claim. Here he finally settled the new colony, which he named "Providence," as providing a place of refuge from injustice and from civil and religious tyranny for the oppressed of all the nations of the earth.

By thus anticipating the Massachusetts Puritans in gaining possession of the much coveted Indian lands, their hostility to him and his colonists became intensified to such a degree, that all commercial as well as friendly intercourse with them was prohibited by penal laws. Williams writes: "They intruded upon the Providence settlers in an unchristianly way, contrary to their own laws and ours." They armed some of the Indians to join the ranks of their soldiers in marching across the border of the colony to seize Samuel Gorton and his associates at Warwick, and to carry them as prisoners to Boston for trial by the chief ministers for alleged blasphemy. It afterward appeared to have been a righteous retribution, that the arms thus put into the hands of the Indians to kill Rhode Islanders, were the first used in King Philip's war against their employers.

The Plymouth colonists joined the Massachusetts aggressors on the east side of Rhode Island, and the Connecticut colonists on the west, to seize the intermediate lands included in the Rhode Island patent. They, with the New Haven colony, formed an alliance under the title of "the Four United Colonies of New England," and while warring against the Indians rigidly excluded the Rhode Island colonists from their alliance and protection. Arnold says: "The surrounding colonies continued their grasping attempts to gain possession of the Indian lands included within the Rhode Island patent."* The sole object of the seizure of Gorton's lands and of his cattle and furniture was to break up his possession and title obtained from Miantonomo. An honest historian of Massachusetts, Judge Savage, records: "I regret to acknowledge the belief is forced upon me that Miantonomo was condemned to death because he favored Gorton and his associates in transferring to them his lands at Pawtuxet." The seizure of Gorton by armed soldiers on the accusation of "blasphemy," was manifestly only a pretence, as evidenced by the final result of his discharge by a majority of two votes of the commissioners of the

* History of Rhode Island, pp. 379-383.

other three colonies, after a year's imprisonment, and by the subsequent order for him to quit Boston within two hours under penalty of death, after he began to address the people there, and narrate to them the wrongs and ruin inflicted on him by their ministers and magistrates. In describing this act of sending a military force to bring Gorton and his companions to Boston to be tried for "blasphemy," and then giving him only two hours' notice to quit under penalty of death for disobedience, Arnold says, page 189: "The details of this memorable trial remind us of the application of a nursery rhyme, as made by the late Archbishop of Dublin:—

> 'Old Father Long-legs wouldn't say his prayers:
> Take him by the right leg—
> Take him by the left leg—
> Take him fast by both legs—
> And throw him down stairs!'

"There, said his Grace, in that nursery verse you may see an epitome of the history of all religious persecutions. Father Long legs refusing to say the prayers that were dictated and ordered by his little tyrants, is regarded as a heretic and suffers martyrdom. Who shall say hereafter that there is no moral conveyed in Mother Goose's melodies?"

As a pretence for seizing the lands of the Indians, the Puritans continued to trump up pecuniary claims against them, in order to levy executions for sale of their property under color of lawful debts due from them. On complaint of a neighboring tribe of Mohegan Indians, Arnold says, page 275: "A great wrong was committed upon the Narragansett Indians by the Commissioners of the Four United Colonies, by levying a fine of five hundred and ninety-five fathoms of wampum-peage as a penalty for alleged offences against other Indian tribes; and by then forcing the chiefs to mortgage their lands to a joint stock company composed of their leading politicians,—Humphrey, Atherton, John Winthrop, Jr., Governor of Connecticut, John Hudson, Richard Smith, Amos Richardson, and others. Then, on default of due payment, the Indians were finally compelled to deliver "formal possession of twig and turf according to English law, in the year 1660." Arnold says they thus attempted to wrench possession of the Indian lands within the Rhode Island charter limits, in order to gain possession of the whole of Rhode Island. This was the foundation of claims persisted in during more than forty years, until finally annulled by special royal commissioners."

Afterward a Narragansett sachem, to avenge the death of Miantonomo by the hands of Uncas, gave notice to the Commissioners of the United Colonies of his intention to make war on the Mohegans. This occasion offered another very favorable opportunity for destroying both tribes, and getting their lands, by joining Uncas with a force of three hundred soldiers, to defeat the more powerful Narragansett chief, Pessicus. Pessicus was then ordered to appear in Boston, and was fined by the Puritans, as the French were fined by the Prussians, for the cost of the war. While in duress he was obliged to sign an agreement to pay two thousand fathoms of wampum within two years. Being unable to pay this imposition when due, "the Four United Colonies sent Humphrey Atherton, with twenty soldiers, pistol in hand, to obtain payment. He forced his way into his wigwam, and seizing him by the hair, dragged him out, threatening instant death if any resistance were made."* A conveyance of his land was made by Pessicus to Atherton, the agent of the joint stock land company, composed of John Winthrop, Jr., the Governor of Connecticut, and others of the principal colonial rulers. Roger Williams states that this company offered him a share of their profits; and he replied, "that the whole transaction was illegal." This same company afterward legally bought lands of the Indian sachems and owners at "Boston Neck" in the Narragansett country, which was sanctioned by the Rhode Island government.

The Connecticut colonists profited as mercenary soldiers under Uncas, and were paid by him in his title deeds to tracts of land. Trumbull states: "Mr. Leffingwell received a conveyance of nearly the whole township of Norwich for his services to Uncas."

King Philip told Mr. John Borden of the wrongs he had suffered, in the following words: "After I became Sachem, the English disarmed all my people, tried them by their judges for damages done by cattle, there being no fences. They assessed damages which they could not pay; and then took their lands. I was seized and confined until I sold tract after tract to pay claims for damages, until only a small part of the dominion of my ancestors remains. I am determined not to live until I have no country."

A plan was devised for obtaining possession of all the Indian lands in the Narragansett country by the Governor of Connecticut, John Winthrop, Jr., by going to England and procuring a new charter for the colony, so altered as to include all the territory previously granted to the Rhode Island colonists by their royal patent. The Colonial Records of Connec-

---

* History of Rhode Island, Arnold, vol. i, p. 199.

ticut show, page 581, that John Winthrop, Jr., went to England in 1662 to obtain a new charter "which should be bounded eastward by the Plymouth line, and northerly by the Massachusetts line." This proposed change of boundary lines, which would have included the whole of Rhode Island, proved to be too open a disregard of the rights of Englishmen under chartered grants, and Winthrop failed in this attempt. Not discouraged in zeal for getting possession of all the Indian lands, the next attempt was to get possession of half of Rhode Island with all the lands of the Narragansett Indians, by obtaining a new charter and surreptitiously interpolating an explanatory description of the east boundary line of Connecticut. The old Connecticut charter defined the east line to be bounded by "Narragansett river," which received its name originally from its forming the division line between Connecticut and the Narragansett country. The new scheme was to be effected by interpolating after the name *Narragansett river*, this super-added explanation: "*commonly called Narragansett Bay*." This bay being twenty-four miles further east than the Narragansett river, now known as the Pawcatuck river, this change would have brought the whole of the Narragansett lands within the jurisdiction of Connecticut. The letters of John Winthrop, Jr., and of his agent in London, John Scott, published in Arnold's History of Rhode Island,* reveal the details of the whole plot, and the employment of a "potent gentleman" and actual bribery to accomplish their purpose of obtaining a new charter with the King's signature, and with this interpolation. Triumphing in this achievement, Connecticut officers were sent to take possession of the Narragansett country under this fraudulent reissue of the Connecticut charter. Arnold says: "The Atherton Company had accomplished their selfish purposes by a baseness that cannot easily be surpassed."

John Clark, the agent in England of the Rhode Island colonists, notified them of these proceedings. They appointed their Deputy Governor, Joseph Jenckes, to make their protest to the royal council in the following words: "Through the private and clandestine deception of the agent of Connecticut, John Winthrop, Jr., the new Connecticut charter is so altered as to bound upon the Narragansett Bay; and this is done contrary to the solemn promise to our agent, Mr. John Clark."†

It is stated: "The King was *surprised* by this interpolation, and commissioners were appointed to rectify the boundary line; so as to nearly

---

* Vol. i, pp. 378-383.   † R. I. Hist. Coll., vol. iii, p. 206.   R. I. Records, iv, p. 276.

coincide with the original charter line of Rhode Island, which was finally confirmed in 1708 by agreement between the two adjacent colonies."

"The evil that men do lives after them"; and the wrong committed by the Puritan rulers of New England, in seizing the lands of Pessicus and transferring them to the Atherton Company, was perpetuated by the latter in attempting to profit by the sale of a portion of them to forty-five families of Huguenots, who were deluded into settling thereon. The Atherton Company contracted with a committee of refugees, who had fled from France after the revocation of the Edict of Nantes, to seek a peaceful asylum in America, where they might freely worship their Creator. In "The History of the Huguenot Settlers in Rhode Island," by the Hon. E. R. Potter, (recently published by Mr. Sidney S. Rider,) it is stated: "The Atherton Company, in the year 1686, contracted 'to lay out A meet and Considerable tract of Land, whereon Each Family shall have a hundred Acres on payment of twenty-five Pounds.' They were located on the border of Narragansett Bay, on land now constituting East Greenwich, and still retaining the name of 'Frenchtown.' They soon built twenty-five houses there, and prepared for a church and school-house, vineyards and orchards; but after finding that the General Assembly of Rhode Island had previously granted the land to others, and that they had been deceived in the validity of the claims of the Atherton Company, they became discouraged, and suffered greatly by being necessitated to become refugees a second time. Some went to New Rochelle, others to New York, where they originated 'The French Church,' that long flourished there. Philadelphia, Virginia, and South Carolina became the abodes of others, where their posterity are respectable inhabitants at the present day. *Allaire* went to New York, *Ayrault* to Newport, *Le Moine* (Mawney), *Tourgé, Collin, Tourtellot, Tourbeaux* (anglicised Tarbox), *Bompasse* (changed to Bumpus and Bump), *Ganeau* (to Gano), Despeau, and a few others, lingered in Rhode Island." The sad breaking up of this Huguenot colony, which promised to become a centre of refinement and civilization, was lamented by Rhode Islanders.

Another Huguenot colony at Oxford, in Massachusetts, was in like manner broken up by Governor Dudley, who gained experience in Indian land speculations by serving on a committee of claims of the Atherton Company. It appears that the leading political Puritans in New England took an active part in profiting by the seizure of the Indian lands; and that Governors Dudley and Stoughton, like Governor Winthrop of Connecticut, made a business of dealing in such acquisitions. Dudley suggested to the General Court of Massachusetts the feasibility of obtaining possession of the Indian lands in the westerly part of the Massachusetts Bay patent, from the Blackstone river to the Connecticut river, by purchase of the tribe of Nipmuck Indians; and was appointed with William Stoughton and Robert Thompson, Colonial Agent on Lands, to make the purchase. The Colonial records show that they obtained a conveyance of the whole Nipmuck country, much larger than the territory of Rhode Island, "for fifty pounds and a black coat," from "Black James," a Nipmuck Indian, and Waban and his tribe of Natic Indians. The Committee were rewarded by a grant of one thousand acres of the land each, for their efficient services.

No question was made of the authority, or right of "Black James," or of the Natic Indians to sell out all the hunting grounds and homes of the adjacent tribe of Nipmuck Indians.

The next move that appears on record, was the petition of Governor Dudley, William Stoughton, a political minister and afterward governor, and Robert Thompson, for a grant of eight square miles of these Indian lands, containing forty-one thousand two hundred and fifty acres. This grant was readily made to them by the General Court of Massachusetts in 1682, (constituting the present township of New Oxford in Worcester county), on the proposed conditions of "the settlement thereon of an orthodox minister and thirty families within four years."

On being notified of this transfer of their hunting grounds and homes, the Nipmuck tribe became exceedingly exasperated, and so hostile to all intruders, that the Land Company, composed of Dudley, Stoughton and Thompson as copartners, could not induce any families to remove and settle on their grant of land within the stipulated term of four years. They consequently obtained an extension of time for three years longer to obtain settlers.

Failing to find any colonists, who knew the circumstances of the grant and the vindictive hostility of the Nipmuck tribe toward all intruders, it became necessary for the copartners to look abroad for emigrants, who were ignorant of the wrong done to the natives, and of their consequent hostility to settlers. The London copartner, Robert Thompson, then had recourse to inveigling some of the families of French refugees, who had fled thither after the revocation of the Edict of Nantes, in 1685, and were seeking a home, where they might peaceably worship their Creator. One Isaac Bertrand du Tuffeau was found willing to attempt enlisting the thirty families required by the terms of the grant. The origin of the

Huguenot Colony, which was settled at Oxford, is stated by one of the principal emigrants; who in after years thus detailed his losses and sufferings in a petition to Governor Shute:—

"Your petitioner humbly begs your Excellency graciously to assist him in his great necessities. Your petitioner, on the revocation of the Edict of Nantes, fled to London, where he was presented by the Treasurer of the Protestant Church of France to the "Society for the propagation of the Gospel among the Indians of New England," of which Mr. Robert Thompson, the President, offered to install him as a member; and also offered land in the government of the Massachusetts Bay. Thereupon, one Isaac Bertrand du Tuffeau desired your petitioner to assist him, the said Du Tuffeau, to go over to New England to settle there a Plantation of the French Refugees. This your petitioner did, by advancing to the said Du Tuffeau the sum of Five hundred Pounds Sterling."

"The said Isaac du Tuffeau, after arriving in Boston with letters of credit from said Major Thompson and your humble petitioner, delivered them to his late excellency Joseph Dudley, Esq., and to the Hon. William Stoughton, deceased; who did grant to the said Du Tuffeau seven hundred and fifty acres of land at New Oxford conjointly with your petitioner." (They thus secured the zeal of the agent by giving him one-half of the land, and at the same time a control of the management.)

"Your petitioner being excited by the letters of said Du Tuffeau, did ship himself and family, with servants, and paid to Captains Foye and Ware passages for above forty persons.

"Your petitioner being arrived at Boston, presented letters from Major Thompson aforesaid to the aforesaid Dudley and Stoughton, Esquires; who were pleased to grant to your petitioner 1750 acres more; and for authentic security, did accompany him to New Oxford, and put him in possession of the said twenty-five hundred acres of land: these he has held for better than thirty years last past, and has spent above Two Thousand Pounds to defend the same from the Indians;—who at divers times have ruined the said plantation and murdered settlers:— Your petitioner most humbly represents that some of the inhabitants do now dispute his right and title, for the purpose of hindering him from the sale of the said plantation; which puts him to the utmost extremity; being now near eighty years of age, and having several children, and children of children depending on him (under God) for subsistence, after having spent more than ten thousand pounds towards the benefit of the country in building ships, making nails, and promoting manufacture of stuffs, hats and resin.

"Your petitioner doth most humbly beg your excellency's compassion in confirming the said two thousand five hundred acres of land free from molestations by the inhabitants and any pretensions of said Du Tuffeau; who abandoned said plantation, selling out the cattle and other movables for *his own* particular use and went to London; where he died in a hospital."

The following authentic details will show how all these troubles were wrongfully brought upon the principal Huguenot settlers, and how the whole Huguenot settlement was broken up and repossessed by Dudley and his copartners.

The records of deeds in Suffolk County, Mass., volume xxx, page 268, show that, on the 24th of May, 1688, Joseph Dudley, William Stoughton, and Robert Thompson signed a deed of twenty-eight hundred and seventy-two acres of land, " selected by said Bertrand du Tuffeau for himself and for Gabriel Bernon within a tract called 'New Oxford Village,' on the condition of building a corn mill thereon and paying a nominal quit rent of forty shillings, New England currency, and with an appended proviso: 'In case of the relinquishment or abandonment of said lands, this grant shall thenceforth cease and be utterly null and void; and the lands shall revert unto the said parties of the First Part, and may be lawfully entered upon by them as their former estate.'"

After the completion of the contract for settling the thirty families and building the mill, the record shows, Feb. 6th, 1690, that all the copartners of the Land Company except Governor Dudley, duly acknowledged the deed before a magistrate, to give it validity; but Governor Dudley withheld both his acknowledgment and the delivery of the deed itself, until the 5th of February, 1716,—a period of twenty-seven years and nine months after it was signed. During all of this time Gabriel Bernon and the thirty refugee families were deprived of a title valid in courts of law. Trespassers upon the land could not be ejected, and the Huguenot settlers here, as in Rhode Island, became disheartened without a legal title. After waiting in vain for three or four years for Dudley's deed, they began to abandon the settlement. Governor Dudley not only withheld his acknowledgment and the delivery of the deed, but encouraged others to dishearten the French families, and cause them to abandon and desert the lands; as appears by his regaining possession of most of the property, mills, and improvements under the clause of the grant providing against abandonment. This deliberately contrived course of Governor Dudley is stated in a remonstrance addressed by Bernon to him, dated March 1, 1707, stating: "Mr. Hagborn, your brother, has done his utmost to ruin my interest in said Oxford. He has caused Cooper to abandon the old mill, and Thomas Allerton to leave my other house, declaring I had no power to settle them. When I made complaint of this, he threatened to drive me from the place, myself." "It is notorious that the said Hagborn, your brother, has caused the planks of my granary to be torn up and conveyed elsewhere, and ordered the oxen to be worked," etc. Superadded to this were the continual annoyances of the surrounding families of Nipmuck Indians, who appear by the remonstrance of the French minister, Daniel Boudet, to the General Court, to have been supplied "with rum without limits, so that they fought like bears with each other." The traders from Boston bought the game and furs they took. Some of the Indians worked as laborers, and the women gathered berries and made baskets and mats for sale.

It appears "the Selectmen of Woodstock, an adjacent town, Petitioned the General Court against the sale of Rum by the Traders; to prevent the riotous drunkenness, and fightings, until they are brought to death's door. There are none here to prevent this woeful conduct."

The Massachusetts rulers having annulled the power of the sachems to maintain order and justice, by granting their lands to the Dudley Land Company, they were left to themselves without any magistrate to restrain them, and literally lawless. Bernon petitioned Governor Dudley, as the ruling member of the Land Company, as well as of the Massachusetts Bay Company, for his aid and influence in restraining the Indians, and only received a letter in reply, dated July 7th, 1702, including the commission of a captain at Oxford, with orders to "take care to arm the people, and garrison them in your *own house*, with a palisade." To quiet the fears of the French settlers at Oxford, Bernon built a strong fort, partly of stone, the ruins of which remain to this day. The alarm at this time was caused by the exodus of most of the Indian families to another distant place. That French emigrants were able to cope with the Indians of America is manifest by their wonderful success in living among the natives-from Quebec to the river Mississippi, where they established themselves permanently before New England was settled. It is to be remembered, too, that when the Johnson family was murdered on Bernon's plantation in 1696, the power of the New England Indians had been nearly annihilated by the war and death of King Philip in 1676, twenty years before, and by the extermination of the Narragansetts and other tribes; so that we have reason to believe that this Huguenot colony in Massachusetts was not broken up by the Indians, but like the Huguenot colony in Rhode Island, by the fraudulent conduct of the Puritan ruler.

Although the border Indians of Canada, during the war between France and England, sent scalping parties to devastate the frontiers of Maine and New York, yet there is no authentic account of their penetrating so far south as Oxford. If the Nipmuck Indians, excited by rum, riotously killed one another, it is not surprising that they may have murdered a family living among them. At the time of the abandonment of Oxford there was no Indian war to threaten the settlers with special danger. This belief is confirmed by the statement of the French minister at Oxford, Daniel Boudet, in his communication to the General Court of Massachusetts, as follows: "The Inhabitants know that all the disturbances that have been in this plantation have happened because some people give the Indians drink without limit. We most humbly supplicate that you give orders to stop this; which puts us in great danger of our lives."

This danger of their lives, by the neglect of the Puritan rulers, and the withholding of their title to their land by the Governor for twenty-seven years and nine months, are sufficient reasons for the dispersion of the Huguenot colony at Oxford

A touching account is given by George T. Daniels, Esq., of the final departure of the body of the colonists from their homes at Oxford:—

"Tradition says, early in the morning of the day of their departure, each family bade adieu to its plantation and home, and then assembled at the church for a season of worship. Next they repaired to the burying ground, to take leave of the graves of departed friends. Finally rejoining in a procession, they went away over the rough forest road to Boston."

"On that August morning in 1696 the scene of leave taking at this sacred spot may be imagined. As we look westward across the meadows, the lonely houses appear with their closed doors and blank windows. Near at hand stands the rude chapel, where just now the farewell songs and prayers have been offered up. In the middle foreground are the graves of the dead; and, here and there, friends bending tearfully over them." — "We shall have to look far in New England history to find an incident more full of dramatic interest and genuine pathos than this."

Describing the conduct of Governor Dudley in withholding the deed of the lands at Oxford nearly twenty-eight years, Mr Daniels remarks: "It will be remembered the deed was drawn May 24, 1688, probably on the completion of the contract to settle the thirty families. Two days after the date of the receipt for building the mill, we find two of the grantors acknowledging the deed before a magistrate; but still it was not delivered   Years passed. The first colony flourished awhile and became extinct; the second was begun and continued five years, was abandoned and lay waste for nine years."\* Then, in 1712, Governor Dudley and the heirs of William Stoughton, the surviving copartners of the Land Company, accomplished their purpose in taking possession of all the lands, with improvements, except the portion on which Bernon had kept tenants for securing uninterrupted possession. They issued "A Proclamation," declaring that: "Having established a number of French Refugees, who have since deserted the place, we do hereby offer to thirty English Families that shall settle thereon, all the lands of the said village, except what is held by possession of Mr. Bernon." "Then the thirty English families came in, took the places of the thirty original French families; and Bernon surrendered to them all his rights to the mills." †

After the departure of the French families, it appears that Bernon struggled to preserve the possession of his houses and land adjacent, by keeping two tenants thereon. To break up also this remaining claim by twenty years' possession, Governor Dudley wrote a letter to Bernon, dated May 20, 1707, threatening to "turn out of the place your two tenants, if you do not remove them yourself"; — with the obvious intent of breaking up his continuous possession, that the plantation might revert to the grantors, under the clause of abandonment.

After narrating the hard-handed dealing of Dudley, Mr. Daniels says: "We cannot avoid the conclusion, that in business matters Bernon had more than his equal in Governor Dudley." ‡

---

\* Page 112.   † Probably to secure the acknowledgment of Dudley.

‡ Page 113, "Huguenots in the Nipmuck Country." The unscrupulous conduct of Governor Dudley, as a predominant Puritan leader and a crafty lawyer, is adverted to by the historian, Bancroft, (vol. iii, pp. 99-100), as remarkable for "profound selfishness." He was denominated "a *wolf*," and Bancroft calls him "Massachusetts' own apostate son." Cotton Mather, who at first admired him for his efficiency in sustaining the ecclesiastical power, and who promoted his appointment to the office of Governor, after finding him to be too selfish, sets him down in his private diary as "A WRETCH."—(Massachusetts Historical Collections.) He addressed a letter to him January 20th, 1707, charging him with "an unhallowed hunger for riches"; with "setting up a reign of bribery, which I know you have been guilty of." "The horrible trade carried on at the castle reaches to

He continues: "At last, after Bernon's hopes and expectations had been again and again disappointed, and he had grown old, and from lack of means unable to assist the settlement further, on Feb. 5th, 1716, nearly twenty-eight years after the deed was written, it was acknowledged by Dudley, and passed over to him." This was done only after Dudley had been deposed by the king and deprived of all further ability to exercise the authority of a Governor to shield his duplicity as a man.

After describing his conduct in the "History of the Huguenots in the Nipmuck Country," Mr. Daniels remarks: "We can hardly withhold our sympathy from Bernon"; "Oxford, as a town, never questioned the rights of Bernon."

After yielding up the legally executed deed to Bernon, Dudley next endeavored to regain the grant at a nominal price, by deterring purchasers from buying it. So effectually did his agents at Oxford exert themselves, that Bernon, in despair, appealed to the sympathies of Dudley's son, in a letter dated October 20th, 1720, as follows: "Sir, I entreat you to assist me in my petition to His Excellency Governor Shute and the General Court, to sustain my title to the Oxford lands. I can make it appear by Major Buor, that when he would have bought my plantation, they told him not to do it; that my title was nothing worth." "I see myself about ruined by such hostility; I entreat you, sir, to aid me in obtaining the assistance of the Governor, your father, that I may sell the lands." He also made efforts to counteract adverse influences by obtaining testimonials in Boston from his "fellow Huguenots, certifying the facts of his paying valuable considerations for the estate, and of his title by possession." Among the twenty or more signers appear the names of J. *Bowdoin*, *Sigourney*, *Daillé*, and *Faneuil*, who married Bernon's sister. At last, on the 16th of March, 1725, a sale of what was left of the original grant was made to Thomas Mayo, Samuel Davis and William Weld for twelve hundred pounds, and thus the Huguenot Colony at Oxford ended.

That religious freedom, the boon sought for by the Huguenots, did not exist in Boston, where Bernon resided while establishing the thirty families of refugees at Oxford, he appears by his diary to have early realized.

the ears of the Lord of Sabaoth," (pp. 130, etc.), adding: "The Attorney-General, your son, has done infamous things in this way." Dr. Increase Mather charges him with gross duplicity, and tells him: "Some you have promoted will say you are the *falsest man in the world*."—(Mass. Hist. Coll., I. Series, vol. iii, pp. 127-8.)

These are samples of a few of the charges made against Dudley by his cotemporaries.

The same intolerance that had shipped back to England the two brothers, Browne, and persecuted non-conformists, was still exercised against dissenters. On refusing to pay a tax for the support of a church which he did not attend, and whose services his people did not understand, it appears by his diary: "They seized, (among other property), my wife's riding hood and my leather breeches" to support Puritanism. In this way he took occasion to make an early protest against taxation for religious sects, and against the union of Church and State. This protest has been in after times sustained by the people of the United States in the first amendment of the national Constitution, and afterward by the people of Massachusetts, in 1834, by the adoption of a Bill of Rights by a popular vote, in the year 1832.

This independent course marked him for a dissenter at once, and incurred the hostility of both the ecclesiastical and civil rulers, causing not only a forfeiture of sympathy for his sufferings as an exile for his faith, but also of his claim to civil rights in his adopted country. This determined his removal to Newport, Rhode Island. This second exile riveted the hostility to him, and to the Huguenot colony at Oxford. At one time, so inveterate were the feelings of the Puritans toward the Rhode Island Colonists, that all commercial intercourse was prohibited with them. One of the earliest acts of the Rhode Island Colonists was a treaty with the Dutch at Manhattan for a supply of necessaries. To get rid of the thirty families of non-conforming Huguenots, Dudley and his associates issued the proclamation for "Thirty English Families to take the places of the thirty French families." At that time Indians and Rhode Islanders stood on a par in the estimation of the Puritans of Massachusetts Bay, neither having any right which was respected by them.

After the arrival of the aged Huguenot in Rhode Island, Mr. Arnold states: "To the persevering piety and untiring zeal of Gabriel Bernon, the first three Episcopal churches in Rhode Island owed their origin,"* viz.: Trinity Church in Newport, the Narragansett Church, and St. John's Church in Providence.

While history shows that the progress of civilization is evidenced by a corresponding progress in the arts of peace and war, from the age of stone to that of bronze, of iron, steel, gunpowder and steam, history does not show that christian virtues and beneficence have correspondingly

* Volume ii, pages 75–116.

kept pace with modern civilization. In the language of Roger Williams: "A depraved appetite for acquisitions of great tracts of land in this wilderness is one of the gods of New England, which the Most High will punish." The punishment is speedily brought about by the reaction of the animal instinct for self-preservation, which exacts prompt vengeance for wrongs, and renders the ways of transgressors proverbially "hard." The millions of losses by the war of the rebellion, as stated by President Lincoln, were the equivalent of the unrequited toil of slaves; and "every drop of blood drawn by the lash, is compensated for by one drawn by the sword." The robbery and murder of the Indians by the Plymouth settlers cost them the lives of half their number by starvation, which might have been saved by friendly intercourse in obtaining a supply from the Indians; and the wrongs done by the Four United Colonies of New England to the natives, cost them the lives of more than fourteen hundred of the settlers and millions of dollars in losses of property, besides the fears and anguish of anticipated vengeance from lurking foes. It was the wrong committed by the Puritan leaders, in robbing Pessicus of his Narragansett lands, "pistol in hand," as described by Arnold, and by transferring them to the Atherton Company, that ruined the forty-five families of the Huguenot Colony in Rhode Island; and the similar transaction in robbing the Nipmuck Indians and granting their lands to political leaders, enabled them to inveigle thirty families of French refugees in London to come to Oxford to fulfill the conditions for holding possession of the Indian lands, with a like disastrous result.

The bold enterprise and vigorous action of our Puritan ancestors would have proved more successful, with less of trouble and suffering, had they adopted for their guidance the Christian instead of the Jewish code.

History has not been silent as to their merits, in making the wilderness to blossom as the rose. We now note their frailties, and the barbarous cruelties of the religious persecution they practiced, only as far as necessary to take warning from their example.

As said by Nathaniel Hawthorne:—"While thanking God for having given us such ancestors, each successive generation may thank Him not less fervently for being one step farther from them in the march of ages." In accordance with this historical estimate, Mr. Charles Sumner advised, in an Address to the City Authorities of Boston: "Cease to vaunt of what you have done, and of what has been done for you; and learn to walk humbly, and think meekly of yourselves."

## STATE OF CIVILIZATION, CUSTOMS AND MODES OF LIVING OF THE INDIANS IN NEW ENGLAND.

The earliest accounts of the natives of North America show that they were an agricultural people, and lived in villages in a rude state of civilization. The first exploring party of the Plymouth settlers found their houses furnished with supplies of corn, beans, tobacco, and other products of agriculture, and with rude materials for manufacture. As previously noticed, the Plymouth settlers first robbed the Indians of corn, and then were furnished by them with seed corn and instructed how to cultivate it. The settlers of Hartford, in Connecticut, obtained a supply of corn when destitute during the first year after their arrival, by sending a sloop around to Narragansett Bay to purchase a cargo from Canonicus. These facts indicate that the natives of New England relied on agriculture as well as on hunting and fishing for their support.

The attempts to produce wheat on the sea-board of New England have not proved successful on account of the open winters in the vicinity of the warm water of the Gulf Stream. Consequently *Indian* corn still constitutes the principal cereal cultivated in New England.

## AGRICULTURE OF THE INDIANS.

The system of agriculture pursued by the Indians is described by Roger Williams as being "a social and loving way of breaking up the land for planting corn. All the men, women and children of a neighborhood join to help speedily with their hoes, made of shells with wooden handles. After the land is broken up, then the women plant and hoe the corn, beans, and *vine apples* called *squash*, which are sweet and wholesome; being a fruit like a young pumpkin, and serving also for bread when corn is exhausted." This account shows that our familiar "squash" is by nature and name a native of Rhode Island. Williams says: "For winter stores the Indians gather chestnuts, hazelnuts, walnuts, and acorns; the latter requiring much soaking and boiling. The walnuts they use both for food and for obtaining an oil for their hair. Strawberries and whortleberries were palatable food freshly gathered; and were dried to make savory corn bread." Wood states in his "New England Prospects": "The Indians excel our farmers in keeping the ground clear with their clam-shell hoes, and hoes made of the shoulder-blades of the moose, as if it were a garden rather than a cornfield. They do not suffer a choking weed to advance its audacious head above their infant corn." Williams says: "The agricultural labors were mostly imposed upon the women; as was also the toil of carrying the burthens of game and fish, taken by their husbands. In the annual removals of their wigwams from the winter residences in sheltered valleys and dense cedar swamps, to the vicinity of their cultivated fields, the wives carry the burthens of the mats and furniture." Williams says: "They are the caterers for their husbands, lugging home deer and other game for belly timber; for a husband will leave a deer to be eaten by wolves rather than impose the load on his own shoulders." He adds: "The mothers, in addition to other burthens, carry about their infant pappooses, wrapped in a beaver's skin and tied to a board two feet long, and one foot broad, with its feet heeled up to its back. The face is left exposed to the cold winds. The mother carries about with her the pappoose when only three or four days old; even when she goes to the clam beds and paddles in the cold water for the clams." Truly the lot of woman was hard in uncivilized life.

In a Canadian Indian village, which I visited in 1820, I saw several pappooses bound to boards set on end and leaned against the side of a cabin, while the mothers made a call within. While I was curiously regarding them, a dog came along, and, from a curiosity like my own to ascertain what they were, ran up to smell of their unprotected faces. Having no use of hands or feet for self defence, all the pappooses could do was to wink and yell when the dog's nose approached their faces. The owners speedily came out to the rescue. During twelve or fifteen months after birth the pappooses are kept most of the time (like the Italian babies) bandaged by swaddling clothes.

## INDIAN HOUSES.

The Indian houses discovered by the Plymouth settlers are described in Mourt's Journal: "They are made round, like an arbor, with long young saplings stuck in the ground and bended over, covered down to the ground with thick and well wrought mats. The door, about a yard high, is made of a suspended mat. An aperture at the top served for a chimney, which is provided also with a covering of a mat to retain the warmth. In the middle of the room are four little crotchets set in the ground, supporting cross-sticks, on which are hung what they have to roast. Around the fire are laid the mats that serve for beds. The frame of poles is double-matted; those within being fairer."

Williams says: "The frames of their houses, constructed of poles, are set in the ground by the men. Then the women cover them with coarse mats, and line the inside with embroidered mats, like a fair show of hangings with us. The mat hung before the opening of the door is lifted aside on entering,"—like the ancient doors of classic Greece and Rome.

To protect these frail houses from the cold blasts of winter, they are removed to sheltered valleys or to dense cedar swamps; wherein they also made their forts, secured by wet ditches. It was to one of these cedar swamps that the Narragansett Indians retreated, and were therein surrounded and exterminated by the four confederated New England colonies; who excluded the Rhode Island people from their confederacy, and purposely left them exposed to extermination by the exasperated Indians.

Williams says: "The Indian houses are removed in a few hours in the summer to the vicinity of the cultivated fields; so that on returning at night to lodge at one of them, it was gone, and I was necessitated to sleep under an adjacent tree." "Their houses are kept warm by fires during the night as well as the day, for avoiding the necessity of warm clothing. Instead of shelves and closets they have baskets to contain their household stuff; and their stores of corn are contained in great hempen bags, capable of holding five or six bushels. They paint their valuable deer and moose skins ornamentally with figures in various colors. The Indian women are ingenious and skillful in braiding mats of flags and corn husks."

I remember several old Indian women who went around to re-seat flag-bottomed chairs with neatness and dexterity, and to sell ornamented baskets and mats.

### INDIAN CLOTHING.

In Summer and Winter, and in their warmed houses, the Indians, as described by Williams, "wear aprons after the pattern of their and our first parents; they have also fur skins on their backs, capable of being readily wrapped about them. A coat or mantle, interwoven curiously with bright colored feathers, is to them what a velvet mantle is to us."

The female children, from their birth, as said by Williams, "they in a modest blush cover with a little apron of a hand breadth." *

---

* Under the more fervent heat of the torrid zone, the Mexican Indians similarly dispense with superfluous clothing, according to the narrative of a traveller, who describes a modern Aztec belle "reposing in a hammock, with no other attire than an elegant diamond ring."

Williams says "the young Indian virgins wear their hair falling down bashfully over their foreheads and eyes," similar to the present fashion of "banging" the hair. Williams testifies to "the always modest behavior of the Indian girls and women in all circumstances of life."

Winslow writes: "On visiting the neighbouring Indians near Plymouth, the women were induced to sell us their coats from their backs, and then, with much shame-facedness, tied leafy boughs about them. Indeed, they are more modest than some of our English women are." "To preserve their fur skins from injury by wet in rains, they economically prefer to wet their own naked skins."

### INDIAN MARRIAGES, AND FAMILY RELATIONSHIPS.

Williams describes the social relationships of the natives as follows: "The Indians generally have only one wife; although there is an inducement to have more, for the profit of their labor. The loss of the labor of daughters to parents is compensated for by customary presents from husbands, as was done in Israel."

Arnold states: "During all the Indian wars the English women, when captured, were uniformly treated with respect, and in not a single instance was violence offered to their persons. Inviolable protection was given with chivalrous honor."

The constant labor and anxiety to procure the means of daily subsistence so continually occupied the time and strength of the men and women, that little leisure was left for the idle dissipation and immoralities that characterize civilized society in modern times.

### DOMESTIC LIFE AMONG THE NATIVES OF THE INTERIOR.

The abundance of food from the shores and fisheries of Narragansett Bay afforded resources to the natives not available to the interior tribes, whose principal supply of food was derived from hunting. An early explorer of the colder regions of the Northwest, occupied by the tribes mainly dependent on the chase for subsistence, gives a graphic account of the toilsome and anxious life of the fathers and mothers having families of children to provide for. The father is described as ever anxious, during the long northern winters, to obtain deer and other wild game. "He goes out at the first gleam of morning light to traverse the snowy forests in pursuit of game, and continues roaming until late in the evening; often returning unsuccessful to his disappointed and faithful wife. She kindly cheers him when thus fatigued and cold, draws off his moccasins,—perhaps wet and stiffened with frost,—and then rubs his feet to restore circulation. She puts away his bow and arrows, and quietly takes a seat by his side in front of the fire. Having no means of satisfying his hunger and that of the family of children, by cooking the expected game, to soothe him she hands him some water to drink and his pipe to smoke. Then his children gather around him lovingly, and a little one climbs on his knee to hear about his hunting wild animals. He tells them he has walked all day long through the woods, but the Great Spirit has sent no deer in his way. To-morrow he might get plenty for them all. Then they retire cheerless, and creep beneath their coverings of skins and furs. The careful wife remains to dry the moccasins and leggings before the fire, and desolately listens to the plaintive tones of the voice of her husband while attempting to sing himself to sleep at midnight, and to obtain rest and strength for renewed toils at the dawn of day."

The Indians of the far West had advantage of abundance of buffalo in their annual summer migrations. In the cold northerly regions the Mohawks obtained scanty supplies of corn from agriculture, and uncertain supplies of game, and consequently, often suffered from destitution, as described by Roger Williams: "Up in the West, two, three and four hundred miles from us, the Mohawks mix the bark of trees with animal fat to satisfy the cravings of hunger, and at times are necessitated to become cannibals. For this reason they are called 'man-eaters,' from the Indian name *Moho*, I eate."

A kind of tuber, growing in the ground like potatoes at the extremities of roots of a shrub, and denoted "ground nuts," varying in size from that of a gooseberry to a hen's egg, afforded a palatable food when boiled or roasted.

#### HOSPITALITY OF THE INDIANS.

Whatever food they obtained was freely shared with less fortunate neighbors; and whoever came in during their meals was invited to participate, even when there was not enough for themselves. Williams says: "When I have arrived in the night the men and their wives have risen to prepare refreshments for me." When banished by the Massachusetts Puritans into the wilderness in mid-winter, he was hospitably received under the roof of Massasoit in Warren, until the return of Spring. Then the kind old chief gave him land for a plantation in Seekonk, near the cove of Ten Mile River. There he planted corn in May, but was warned again to leave the jurisdiction of Massachusetts. He then went around to another place at the mouth of Moshassuck river, which was freely presented to him by the Narragansett chief Canonicus. There he founded the colony of Providence Plantations, where we now are.

The debt of gratitude due to the good old chief Massasoit as a benefactor to the founder of our State has recently been recognized by the people of Warren, who are engaged in erecting a monument to him.*

When justly and kindly treated it appears that the Indians on the shores of Narragansett Bay have been friendly and gentle toward the European settlers. Williams says: "I have been gratefully requited for kindnesses rendered to Indians, many years after I had forgotten them. They lovingly greet the English in the woods on meeting them, and also each other, by the word 'Netop,'— friend." "They enjoy stopping to chat with one another in their forest paths, and will strike a fire with stones or sticks and take a smoke together." This description of their friendly meetings affords a contrast to their unfriendly meetings with the maritime adventurers from Europe, "who visited every convenient port of the present United States to capture Indians for slaves,"— as affirmed by Mr. Bancroft, and as narrated by Morton in the History of Plymouth; who says the spot where the settlers first met the Indians was called by the name of "First Encounter" with the Enemy.

The Indians had their annual festivals after harvest, corresponding with Thanksgiving, which custom may have been the example copied by the New England settlers. Williams says: "The Indians showed their grateful feelings by shoutings for their bountiful god, Cowtautowit, and made general distribution of presents, corresponding with Christmas presents with us." They had their social gatherings. The great Council House of the Narragansetts was fifty feet in diameter. They delighted to assemble in general meetings in temporary structures of arbors, one or two hundred feet long. There they had public games and amusements. In their public councils they are seated in a circle, commonly around a fire, hence denoted "the council fire." They formed several circles to listen to the news, and hear debates on business affairs. It appears the

---

* In noticing this beneficent work, the editor of a Cincinnati journal remarks: "While the people of Rhode Island are preparing a monument for the Indians, the people of Colorado are preparing Indians for a monument."

women attended some of these council debates, and influenced decisions. After deciding trials of wrong doers, their punishments were inflicted by the hands of the Sachems as the executive rulers.

### RELIGION.

The Indians believed in the existence of a Great Spirit, denominated Manitou, and in an all-pervading diffusion of a portion of this intelligence in living animals, and even in lifeless material objects, somewhat corresponding with Greek and Roman mythology. Williams satirically remarks: "Like the Papists, they have their He and She Saints, as Saint Patrick, Saint Dennis. They have their Fire God, who leaps in a spark out of a stone, to warm a poor Indian, to cook his food, and burn him when he offends." "They have a good custom not to disturb any one in their religious worship." What a blessing it might have been had the first settlers of New England adopted this Indian custom?

A contentment with their humble lot prevailed, according to Williams's account of their creeping thankfully at night into a coat of fur skins, counting it a felicity to be snug therein.

### INDIAN LANGUAGES.

It is stated the Indian languages were remarkably copious, regular in inflections, and diversified by combining words together. Four dialects existed in North America,—the Esquimaux and Delaware, spoken on the sea-coast, the Iroquois in the interior. The Delaware language was spoken throughout several hundreds of miles north and south of Rhode Island.

To open missionary communications with the natives, Eliot translated the Bible into the Indian language of New England, with unwearied zeal; and Roger Williams wrote an Indian dictionary, which he entitled "A Key to the Languages of America," and it now constitutes one of the most instructive works relating to Indian history.

### INDIAN MANUFACTURES AND TRADES.

The Narragansett Indians are described by Wood, an early historical writer, as being "the most numerous as well as the most industrious and richest of the Indian tribes. They catch beavers, otters and musquashes for furs to sell to the English, and receive commodities which they sell to remote Indians for double profit. They seek rather to grow rich by industry than to become famous in war. Some make bows and arrows, wooden dishes, and earthen vessels and pipes. Some on the Bay shore store up shells in summer for making wampum money in winter. They dressed the skins of animals to serve as leather (commonly produced by tanning) by using the brains of animals instead of oak bark. Their snow shoes were copied by European settlers for their usefulness "

"Narragansett," says Wood, "is the manufactory of all kinds of rude merchandize for the Indians of those parts, especially great stone pipes holding a quarter of an ounce of tobacco. With the steel awl-blades they obtain from the Dutch and English they perforate the stems with such excellent art in imitating English pipes of green stone, that it is hard to distinguish the difference. Some of the stone pipes carved are so massy that a man might be hurt by one of them falling upon him; and swung by the stem might be sufficient to beat out the brains of an ass." He adds this moral reflection: " How many men's brains are smoked out, and asses' brains smoked in by tobacco pipes in England." Another old writer adds: "They account it odious for boys to smoke, while our young men often smoke, not being so well trained."

The Calumet of Peace is described by Hennepin as "a large tobacco pipe of red, black or white stone, with the bowl finely polished, and a stem or reed of cane two feet and a half long, adorned with bright colored feathers, interlaced with women's hair." "This pipe is a safe conduct among all the allies of the nation, which furnishes the calumet as a symbol of peace."

The arrow-heads, hatchets, and other stone implements found in Ohio, are described by Mr. Atwater to be precisely similar to those found in all the Atlantic States. Plates of copper, copper pipe tube, and silver articles have been found in the works of the mound builders of the Mississippi valley. These relics are supposed to have been procured from the copper mines of Lake Superior, and probably some of the pots and earthen vessels were obtained from the spoils of the Aztecs in Mexico by these northern invaders.

The material of flint stone for arrow-heads, I believe, is found nowhere in New England except on the northern border of Moosehead Lake in Maine. There the precipitous Mount Kineo, two thousand feet above the level of the sea, is composed of a vast mass of pure flint stone.

"Tomahawks" were originally made somewhat resembling the South Sea Island clubs, terminating in a heavy knob; and flint hatchets were originally used in warfare before the introduction of the steel implements by Europeans.

### THE INDIAN MODES OF TRAVELLING, AND TRANSMITTING INTELLIGENCE.

"For speedily transmitting important intelligence the Indian messengers run swiftly; and at every town fresh messengers are speeded away to reach the chief's house. When within a mile the messenger commences hallooing, and all who hear begin to halloo; whereby a great concourse is soon gathered to hear the news; for all men have an itching desire for news." Williams continues: "It is admirable to see what smooth paths their naked, hardened feet have worn in trails leading through the wilderness, even among stony places. Guides and porters are found for hire to conduct to remote hunting-houses for lodging in the vast forests at night. I have often been lost in the woods and guided by them. The Indians are quick of foot, being from boyhood trained to practice running. To save the wear of shoes they often carry them on their backs. I have known Indian messengers to run four score to an hundred miles in a summer day, and return in two days afterwards."

These feats of pedestrianism excel modern walking matches, when it is considered that the Indian trails were uneven forest pathways. They demonstrate that men can walk one hundred miles per day. Williams states: "Notwithstanding their agility the natives covet the possession of horses more than of cattle and cows; preferring," as he quaintly says, "the comfort of ease to their legs to that of the belly from milk."

"They are punctual to their appointments, and have sometimes charged me with a lie for failing to keep time punctually with appointments."

"In conversation they have often asked me why came the Englishman here? Is it because you want wood for fire? When they have burnt up the wood around them, they are faine to remove to a fresh place to get more."

### INDIAN CANOES AND FISHERIES.

In traversing the rivers as well as forests the natives were active and expert; and even adventured on the ocean waves in fleets of canoes. Williams affirms: "They had naval conflicts of thirty or forty canoes on each side. I have divers times been aided by them in crossing rivers and bays. They harpoon sturgeons and kill bass with arrows from their canoes, after cooping them in some little cove or river by nets."

The Narragansetts made canoes of large chestnut, white wood, and trunks of pine trees, hollowed out by stone adzes and chisels, and by burning out the middle part and scraping the charred surface. To accomplish the labor ten or twelve days and much skill are requisite, and consequently a large "dug out" canoe was prized as valuable property. The Canadian and eastern Indians had recourse to the thin sheets of bark stripped from the peculiar kind of birch which abounds in those regions, and serves to form sheets that were sewed together, and rendered water tight by turpentine or pitch. These sheets being sewed by withs and deer-sinews to ribs of bended hoops of wood, were so light as to be readily transported from the sources of adjacent rivers across ridges, denoted "carrying places"; so that there were thus established regular lines of communication by water for transferring furs and food, (like those of modern civilization,) by "the *coureurs des bois.*"

Father Hennepin explored the wild regions of the West by journeys of thousands of miles, as he states, "in small canoes made of bark of birch trees, carrying nothing with me but a blanket and a mat of rushes, which served as bed and quilt."

Williams says: "The sea-board Indians made their dug out canoes sufficiently large for carrying forty men, who propelled them by paddles, and by sails made of mats upheld by poles for masts. In them they crossed the sea to Block Island.

### INDIAN MONEY, OR WAMPUM-PEAGE.

The currency adopted by the natives of New England to represent interchangeable values, denominated wampum, was manufactured from sea shells, somewhat after the Asiatic models of perforated discs of metal, to be strung like beads for readiness of handling and counting. The Narragansett Indians being skillful in making arrow-heads, pots, hatchets and other articles of commerce, and having intercourse with the Dutch for distributing European commodities among the Indians of the interior, appear to have taken the lead in establishing a kind of currency for estimating values by a common money standard. They gathered the shells in summer and employed their leisure time in winter in rounding the pieces of shells into little discs, and making small holes through the middle of them for stringing them together. The conical apex of the periwinkle shell served to facilitate the work of rounding the edges and making the hole through the middle. The circular discs thus made constituted the *white* wampum, and from the facility of manufacture was estimated at only half of the value of the dark or blue wampum, made of the central part of the quahog shell. When the Dutch furnished the steel awl-blades to the natives for perforating the holes through the solid shell, the dark blue wampum was more easily made than before. The white wampum was estimated at only half of the current value of the black wampum. Both were strung on deer's sinews, and estimated at a certain number per foot or fathom.

Williams says: "Six of the small white beads, with holes to string them like bracelets, are current with the English for one penny, and three of the black ones, inclining to blue, make an English penny." "The white they call *Wampum*, the black *Suckahoc*." "When strung or wrought into girdles they are denoted *Wampum-peage*."

"Before ever the Indians had awl-blades from Europe they made shift to bore holes in their shell money with stone, such as used with wooden handles to fell trees."

In the early history of New England frequent mention is made of purchases of land, etc., for a certain number of fathoms of wampum; but I have been unable to find a specification of any standard number of shells or coins contained on a string of six feet, or one fathom. To obtain an estimate of the probable number I had recourse to measuring the thickness of each disc in the most perfect specimens now obtainable.

There appears to be a diversity of dimensions of the discs, as might be expected from the rude process originally employed to grind them by hand on the surfaces of stones. In this respect they are much less uniform than coins from steel dies. Some coarse specimens are found nearly half an inch thick, and others about one-fourth and three-sixteenths of an inch; and the diameters about five-sixteenths of an inch. To obtain the most authentic average dimensions of these little primitive coins I measured a fac-simile engraving of "the William Penn Wampum Belt," on which there appear to be very nearly five hundred in one fathom; so that probably a standard fathom of wampum represented half a thousand coined shells.

The remarkable resemblance between the shell wampum beads made in Rhode Island and in the islands of the Pacific ocean, attracted my attention. Those made by the South Sea Islanders are very perfect and even ornamental as strings of beads for bracelets and necklaces. They also are made of black and white colors; the former being of only one-fourth the thickness of the latter, and of the uniform diameter of one-fifth of an inch, pierced with very small central holes. About eighteen hundred of the white shell discs make a string of one fathom, and nearly four thousand of the black. The beauty of this fine shell work, with interlaced black and white beads fancifully arranged, seems to indicate their use for ornament rather than money.

The black and white shell beads were interwoven on strings, ornamentally, to form belts and bracelets, which were worn by the men and women, and, like diamonds, represented the wealth of the wearer. Captain Church gives a graphic account of the belts and circlets of wampum which constituted the regalia of King Philip, delivered up by Anawan, after his capture. Captain Church states that the belts were tastefully wrought in black and white into figures of birds and animals, with fanciful border designs. Williams describes an elaborate wampum belt woven of the width of several inches, and valued at more than ten pounds.

Wood states: "The wealthy natives preserve their wampum with anxiety and care as their wealth. The wealthy natives having no strong chests for securing this kind of wealth or money, carefully wore their wampum constantly in the day time. At night they keep it under their heads while they sleep." Thus the care of riches were even more burthensome to the Indians than to modern capitalists, who have their iron chests and vaults.

These traits of Indian character for economy and thrift are evidences of their capability of taking care of themselves, were they allowed a fair chance under the protection of courts of justice and a police, like that established in the British dominion in Canada, as described in Governor Laird's speech to the Indians at Fort McLeod in 1877, in the following words:—

"If you sign the treaty for the sale of your lands, every man, woman and child will get twelve dollars each, paid to the head of the family; and ever afterwards each Indian will get five dollars. Chiefs will get a suit of clothes, a silver medal and flag; and every third year another suit of clothes. To every five persons one square mile will be allotted as a reserve, from which all trespassers will be excluded. Roads will be made, cattle given, and potatoes for planting; and as soon as you make a settlement teachers will be sent to instruct your children." "You all know you can rely on the Queen's promises being fulfilled, for no promise to you has ever been broken." *

"The Indian chiefs replied: 'Your treatment of us has always been good. If you had not sent the Police to our country, bad men would have killed us with whiskey, and what should we all have been this day?'"

A similar equitable system has been magnanimously adopted by British rulers in Australia.

By paying each individual for improvements made, and an equitable compensation for loss of hunting grounds, if the reckless and dissolute fail to retain their property, the fault will be their own, and not imputable to the rapacity of the political financiers of a great Republic, who place the natives under guardianship, and entail their property for the future profit of the Republic by removing them from one reservation to another less valuable, until they are exterminated by trespassers. While the sons of rich white men are purposely left free to squander their inheritance under special laws against entailments, tending to perpetuate a money aristocracy under a democratic form of government, the sons of the Red men are strictly restrained from selling their lands, and discouraged from hopes

---

*This system of justice and good faith was originally adopted by the founder of the State of Rhode Island in obtaining lands from the Indians, with the result of the most kindly intercourse with them, until the Four United Colonies commenced a war of extermination against them. In a letter to the Commissioners of these Colonies, dated in 1767, he explains his just and peaceful intercourse with the natives, as follows:—

"I mortgaged my house in Salem (worth some hundreds) for supplies of gifts to Massasoit,—yea, and to all his; and also to Canounicus and all his, in tokens and presents, many years before I came in person to Narragansett. And when I arrived, I was welcomed by both of them." "I also bore the charges and venture of all gratuities, which I gave to the great Sachems round about us, and to a peaceable and loving neighborhood lay engaged for my great charge and travel among them." (Backus, vol. I, p. 94.) After the death of Williams, his son stated in a letter: "My father gave away all; and being ancient, his needs must pinch somewhere. He gave to me only about three acres of land. It looked hard, that out of so much at his disposal, he should have had so little." Governor Winslow, on visiting Williams, in Providence, as noticed in a letter written to Major Mason, "kindly melted, and put a piece of gold into the hands of my wife for the supply of our necessities."

This self-denying spirit of true christian beneficence was the means of subduing the natives to reciprocal acts of kindness, and of breaking up an alliance between the Pequots and Narragansetts against the Four United Colonies, which would have swept away nearly all the European settlers of New England. In the final war of King Philip he went safely amid the army of exasperated warriors, and extorted from them this precious eulogium: "You are a good man, and not a hair of your head shall be injured."

of bettering their condition by economy and industry. A gradual extermination of the race is the sure result.

The Puritan rulers of the Four United Colonies contrived to gain possession of the much coveted Narragansett lands under the pretence of involving the sachems in debt, payable in wampum, their own coin; and then, in default of payment, they levied on their lands by a process of civil execution, instead of military conquest; this being a quieter way of accomplishing their purpose. As previously noticed, the rulers took advantage of inciting Uncas to attack the Narragansetts, and took their pay in deeds of lands. Then when the Narragansetts made war in retaliation, the colonists sent three hundred soldiers to arrest him, and then fined him for the costs, as the Prussians did the French, and imposed a fine of two thousand fathoms of wampum, equal to more than two miles in length of coins. The poor sachem being unable to produce such a quantity, was made to sign a bond and mortgage, and then in default to surrender his land as previously stated. This was truly a Shylock plan of procedure; but the injustice was checked and the proceedings annulled by the royal commissioners.

Calculating the number of white wampum at five hundred to the fathom, Pessicus was fined a million of the shell coins, payable at a short credit.

Williams refers to the financial abilities of some of the natives as follows: "'Tis admirable how quick the Indians are in casting up great numbers, without the help of letters, figures, or pens, by using grains of corn. They are subtle in bargains, and will try different markets, going thirty miles to save a sixpence."

"Some are honest, but most of them will never pay a debt unless followed up to their houses. They partake of the general folly of mankind, by running into tormenting debts, not only for necessary, but also for unnecessary things."

The measures of the time of day, were designated by the position of the sun in the heavens. The number of days by "suns," of months by "moons," and years by "Winter snows or harvests."

### FORMS OF INDIAN GOVERNMENT.

The tribal system of Indian government was necessarily democratic, and somewhat paternal. Councils of the people were held for consultation, at which it appears the women were sometimes present, on the conveyance of lands and making treaties. The chiefs rarely acted in making laws and regulating tribal affairs, without convening the people for their assent and ratification. Their "ayes and nays" were expressed by peculiar guttural sounds, corresponding with cheering and the goose-like hissings in modern popular assemblies. The executive functions were performed by the sachems; and also the duties of a sheriff in punishing criminals devolved upon them. They did not lack debaters in their discussions or *powwows*, and discords occurred like those in our modern assemblies of the people.

### MEDICAL PRACTICE OF THE INDIANS.

The Indians, having no experience with chemical compounds, confined their treatment of the sick to herbs and roots in doctoring. As described by Mr. Douglas: "They pursued the old women's treatment as practised in country villages in England in ancient times, by using decoctions of vegetables for emetics, for cathartics, and sudorifics. The use of steam baths in caves, or beneath mats, by heating stones and pouring water thereon, was deemed a health restoring expedient. But with little reliance on human skill, the superstitious natives placed more hope on the spiritual influence of their religious quack doctors, or Powwow men, who performed mystical ceremonies over invalids with shoutings and howlings, as if to scare away affrighted demons of diseases. Their services were paid for like lawyers' fees, the amount paid being also in proportion to the continuance of vociferations.

### FISHING AND HUNTING.

The abundance of fish in the Bay, and the wild game on the land, formed a principal part of the subsistence of the Narragansett Indians. They used nets made of twisted fibres of hemp, and of deer's sinews; and fish-hooks made of sharpened bones of birds and of certain fish bones. Williams says: "They were dexterous in using scoop nets and in spearing fishes in the night by alluring them to the surface by the glare of light from burning torches placed in front of their canoes. They were successful in catching the several kinds of fish still found in the Bay, and known by their Indian names of tautog and scuppaug. Bass, and smaller fish called smelt and frost fish were perseveringly sought for by night and by day. "They patiently lie down with their nearly naked bodies on the cold shores, and wade in icy water to set their nets."

The clam-bakes on the shores of Narragansett Bay were as much appreciated and enjoyed by the natives in former days, as by the present multitudes of excursionists. Williams describes clams as "a sweet kind of shell-fish, readily digged out from the shore-sands at low water by the women, and delightfully relished by all Indians for the savory broth made by them, which serves instead of salt for seasoning their nassaump and corn bread."

Williams adds: "The Indian women and English swine go to the shores at low water to dig and root out the clams, and are competitors. The swine are therefore hated by the Indian women."

"The English have learned to make a dainty dish of the brains of a bass, resembling marrow."

### INDIAN COOKERY AND INDIAN BREAD.

"To kindle a fire for cooking, the natives strike violently together two stones, with some punk intervening between them. After kindling a fire, they place therein several stones or boulders in a layer; and after becoming hot the stones are dropped in water containing fish or flesh in a wooden vessel, thus causing the water to boil. The soapstone pots were in like manner placed in a fire until they became hot, and then the water was poured in and the food to be boiled was placed therein."

The original mode of Indian cookery, by heating stones, is still practised by the shore parties at their picnics on the borders of Narragansett Bay. The heated stones are arranged like a pavement on the ground, some sea-weed is spread upon them, and then layers of clams, fish, ears of corn, potatoes, and other articles of food, are added in successive layers, until a little mound is raised, with a thick covering of sea-weed. Then a pailful of water, dashed upon the top of it, percolates to the hot stones, and produces abundance of steam, that is diffused throughout the whole mass. After a suitable time the mound is opened and the contents carefully withdrawn and served on the festive board. Some little practice is requisite before novices and dainty young ladies can gracefully lift the clam from its native shell by the neck, and suspend it on a poise above the parted lips, with the face and eyes turned heavenward, as if with pious devotion to the idolized clam.

To reduce the flinty kernels of corn to meal for making bread, the Indians use the stone pestles, such as are here exhibited before you. Previously to the introduction of mill-stones, wooden pestles shod with iron and lifted by water wheels, were used by the pioneers, and denominated " Stamping Mills." The first water-wheel made in Rhode Island, soon after the arrival of Williams, was for a stamping mill near Steven's bridge on the Moshassuck river. The street leading to that place still bears the descriptive name of " Stamper Street." The water privilege below was given by the original proprietors to John Smith in consideration of his building thereon a mill for grinding corn. The first mill built in Massachusetts was for grinding corn at Plymouth in 1636, as appears by the colonial records.

The Indians rendered the corn more brittle for being pulverized by pestles, and at the same time prepared for eating, by parching it in hot ashes, and then sifting it out. Like modern "pop-corn" this parched meal was ready cooked for food, and required only to be moistened with water. Williams says: "I have made many a good dinner and supper of parched meal, moistened by a spoonful of water from a brook. With no other food I have travelled with two hundred Indians an hundred miles; each one carrying a hollow leather girdle around his waist, or a little basket on his back, filled with parched meal."

This parched meal, kneaded with water, and baked on a hot stone, or before a fire, constituted the bread they called "*Nokik*,"— strangely anglicised into *No Cake*. The unparched meal makes Journey Cake, or Johnny Cake. In his description of the mode of making a Johnny Cake, Roger Williams omits an essential part of the preliminary process, which requires the use of *boiling* water instead of *cold* water in kneading the meal. This knowledge was acquired by me, under peculiar difficulties, while floating down the Ohio river from Pittsburgh to Cincinnati on a flat boat or ark in 1817, before steamboats were in use there. Our party bought a boat and were their own navigators and cooks. To our surprise and indignation our first Johnny Cake became meal again when baked before the fire. To learn the art and mystery, I rowed the skiff from the flat boat to a house on the shore, and there under the instruction of the smiling wife of an Ohio farmer, I finished my scientific education in this special department. She poured *boiling* water upon the corn meal, and invited me to test the quality by partaking of the cake. Some of the gentlemen here present may be as ignorant as I was, and, profiting by this lesson, may leave the hall wiser if not better men.

The introduction, by Europeans, of light metallic kettles, adapted for being hung over a fire, afforded desirable facilities for convenience of transportation, and for more quickly boiling food in traversing wild forests.

An opportunity was afforded of inspecting the process of cooking in these kettles by a party of Sioux Indians, near the Falls of St. Anthony, in the year 1847. A war party, returning from an attack on a tribe of Chippeway Indians, had erected their lodges on the banks of the Mississippi river. The captain of the steamboat landed a few of us to visit the encampment of the painted warriors beneath the shade of the forests. They exhibited a surprising spectacle with their peculiar attire, vermillion streaked faces, and feathers in their hair. Many of them were gathered around their boiling pots suspended over blazing fires, resembling the weird scene of the witches' caldron in Macbeth. They severally contributed to the boiling caldrons such articles as they had procured from the forest and river. The whirling ebullition of this boiling compound brought to light successively the materials of which the soup was composed; showing the bill of fare to be pieces of meat, fish, and whole turtles, that seemed swimming amid the boiling currents. The view of this compound was sufficient to cure the appetite of a hungry Englishman.

The lodges were made by inserting four poles in the ground, about twelve feet apart, and by tying their inclined tops together, and then leaning additional poles to rest against the tops of the four standard poles, with the lower ends spread out to a circle at the bottom. Buffalo skins sewed together in large sheets were wrapped around the conical frames of the poles, and a rope wound spirally around the outside, like hoops, bound them all tightly together. The outsides of the skins were painted with figures of animals. Some few presents made to the Indians conciliated them to acts of courtesy instead of scalping. One of the stalwart plumed warriors gallantly advanced toward a beautiful St. Louis belle, and making a formal bow, took an eagle's feather from his hair, and chivalrously inserted it in the tresses of the confused and blushing girl. Pausing a moment to gaze admiringly upon her, and making another formal bow, he slowly turned and strode away to rejoin his wild companions.

This tribe of Sioux were compelled by the United States government to pay a penalty to the tribe of Chippeway Indians for this assault upon them.

MOURNINGS FOR THE DEAD.

That the natives of New England had kindly feelings and affections, was manifested by their sensibilities for the death of friends. Williams says: "When they come to the grave they lay the body down. Then all join in lamentations. I have seen tears run down the cheeks of stoutest captains as well as of little children. After the body is laid in the grave, sometimes personal effects are deposited with it, as a solemn sacrifice. On the death of his son, I saw the aged chief, Canonicus, as a great sacrifice to him, burn his residence. Their mourning is continued for months."

Black appears to have been selected for an emblem of grief, as devoid of cheerful radiance and reflection of light, alike by the natives of Europe and America. The Indians used soot mingled with oil for consistency as a pigment. The memory of the dead was cherished, as manifest by the return of the Indians at times to visit and honor the graves of their fathers. Now the mourners and their graves have disappeared, except in the far West, where the mounds, like the pyramids, have survived as memorials of the builders.

> "They grieved;—but no wail from their slumbers may come;
> They joyed: but the voice of their gladness is done.
> They died,—aye they died; and we things that are now,
> Who walk on the turf that lies over their brow,
> Who make in their dwellings our transient abode,—
> Meet the changes they met in their pilgrimage road"

We now occupy their places for our transient abode, as others will soon succeed us, and make in our dwellings their equally transient abode.

These fleeting scenes of continual changes in our pilgrimage road, constitute the history of mankind. To preserve memorials of the race of Red men, who once owned and occupied the pleasant shores of Narragansett Bay, now our enjoyable homes, is a special object and duty of the members of our Historical Society, as has been set forth by our esteemed associate, Mr. Denison:—

> "We, children of a favored day,
> Inheriting their homes,
> Would guard their history from decay,
> And mark their mouldering tombs."

# INDEX.

|  | PAGE. |
|---|---|
| Allen, Zachariah, Address by on the conditions of life, habits and customs of the native Indians of America, and their treatment by the first settlers | 97–151 |
| An early proclamation | 62, 63 |

Bower, Samuel J., notice of..................................70, 71

Charter, amendment of..........................................20
Committee to disburse State appropriation......................20
Communication from Rev. Frederic Denison......................30
Changes in a hundred years..................................61, 62

Donations................................13, 14, 16, 18, 19, 23, 26, 30

GENEALOGIES:—

    Genealogies and Estates in Charlestown, Mass..............53
    Whitney Family, by Stephen Whitney Phœnix..................54
    Dunster Family, by Samuel Dunster...........................55
    Russell Family, by John R. Bartlett...........................55
    Drowne Family, by Henry Thayer Drowne......................55
    Cooke Family, by Albert R. Cooke.............................55
    Tilley Family, by R. Hammitt Tilley............................55
    Douglas Family, by Charles H. J. Douglas....................55

|                                                                              | PAGE. |
|---|---|
| Hitchcock, Rev. Dr., oration by                                              | 68, 69 |
| Herlitz, Mrs. Louisa Lippitt, letter from                                    | 18 |
| "        "        "        " watch presented to Historical Society, by      | 56 |
| Independence, Declaration of in Providence                                   | 64–65 |
| "        commemoration of, 1826                                              | 69–73 |
| Liberty granted Mr. Henry T. Beckwith to copy an engraving                   | 24 |
| "        "   Rev. Mr. Stone to photograph the sword and pistols that were owned and used by Col. Ephraim Bowen in the Revolution | 28 |
| Librarian authorized to examine manuscripts offered for sale to the Society by Mr. James C. Mauran, of Newport | 36 |

MEMBERS:—

| Honorary | 5 |
|---|---|
| Corresponding | 6–7 |
| Resident | 8–11 |
| Life | 12 |
| Resident, elected | 19, 23, 26, 44 |
| Corresponding, elected | 19, 26, 44 |
| Honorary, elected | 19, 23, 44 |
| Life, elected | 26 |

NECROLOGY:—

| Williams, William G. | 85, 86 |
|---|---|
| Easton, Nicholas Redwood | 86, 87 |
| Paine, Walter | 87, 88 |
| Grosvenor, Col. Robert | 88 |
| Spicer, George Thurston | 89–91 |
| Oldfield, John | 91 |
| Pabodie, Benjamin Gladding | 92, 93 |
| Arnold, Hon. Samuel G. | 93–96 |

# INDEX.

| | PAGE. |
|---|---|
| Officers of the Society | 3-4 |
| Ode, semi-centennial, by Albert G. Greene | 71, 72 |

| | |
|---|---|
| Proceedings, with various reports to be printed | 21-46 |
| Proposed amendments to the Constitution indefinitely postponed | 24 |
| Purchase of Rider's Historical Tracts authorized | 28 |
| Papers read | 52, 53 |
| Patriotic Song | 67 |

Request for loan of plan of Camp Sprague granted............40
RESOLUTIONS :—
   Proffering co-operation and aid in observing the bi-centennial anniversary of the Settlement of Bristol..........25
   Thanks to Gen. Horatio Rogers............32
      " William B. Weeden............42
      " Hon. William D. Brayton............41
      " Dr. E. M. Snow and S. S. Rider............44
REPORTS :—
   Committee on the Angell-Johnston Indian Pottery Development............36-39
   Treasurer............49-51
   Librarian............52-75
   Procurator for Newport............76-77
     " Bristol............78-79
   Committee on Grounds and Building............80
     " " Genealogical Researches ............81-82
     " " Publications............83
     " " State appropriation............84

Thanks voted to Special Committee............21
   " " " Stephen Whitney Phœnix............27
   " " " Mrs. John Carter Brown............27

Williams, William G., resolution concerning ............19
Washington Bridge, notice of............57
Wants of the Society............73-75

www.ingramcontent.com/pod-product-compliance
Lightning Source LLC
Chambersburg PA
CBHW030336170426
43202CB00010B/1140